In the Foreign Legion

In the Foreign Legion

The Experiences of a Journalist
Who Joined the French Foreign Legion
in North Africa at the
Turn of the 20th Century

Erwin Rosen

LEONAUR

In the Foreign Legion
The Experiences of a Journalist Who Joined the French Foreign Legion
in North Africa at the Turn of the 20th Century
by Erwin Rosen

First published under the title
In the Foreign Legion

Leonaur is an imprint
of Oakpast Ltd

ISBN: 978-0-85706-387-8 (hardcover)
ISBN: 978-0-85706-388-5 (softcover)

http://www.leonaur.com

Publisher's Notes

The opinions of the authors represent a view of events in which he
was a participant related from his own perspective,
as such the text is relevant as an historical document.

The views expressed in this book are not necessarily
those of the publisher.

Contents

Prologue

Once upon a time there was a young student at a German University who found life too fresh, too joyous, to care very much for professors and college halls. Parental objections he disregarded. Things came to a climax. And the very next *Schnelldampfer* had amongst its passengers a boy in disgrace, bound for the country of unlimited possibilities in search of a fortune. . . .

The boy did not see very much of fortune, but met with a great deal of hard work. His father did not consider New York a suitable place for bad boys, and booked him a through passage to Galveston. There the ex-student contracted hotel bills, feeling very much out of place, until a man who took a fancy to him gave him a job on a farm in Texas. There the boy learnt a good deal about riding and shooting, but rather less about cotton raising. This was the beginning. In the course of time he became translator of Associated Press Despatches for a big German paper in St. Louis and started in newspaper life.

From vast New York to the Golden Gate his new profession carried him: he was sent as a war correspondent to Cuba, he learned wisdom from the kings of journalism, he paid flying visits to small Central American republics whenever a new little revolution was in sight. Incidentally he acquired a taste for adventure. Then the boy, a man now, was called back to the Fatherland, to be a journalist, editor and novelist. He was fairly successful. And a woman's love came into his life. . . .

But he lost the jewel happiness. The continual fight for existence and battling for daily bread of his American career, so full of ups and downs, was hardly a good preparation for quiet respectability. Wise men called him a fool, a fool unspeakable, who squandered his talents in light-heartedness. And finally a time came when even his wife to be could no more believe in him. The jewel happiness was lost. . . .

The man at any rate recognised his loss; he recognised that life was no longer worth living. A dull feeling of hopelessness came over him. And in his hour of despair he remembered the blood of adventure in his veins. A wild life he would have: he would forget.

He enlisted as a soldier in the French Foreign Legion.

That man was I. I had burned my boats behind me. Not a soul knew where I was. Those who loved me should think that I was dead. I lived the hard life of a *légionnaire*; I had no hopes, no aspirations, no thought for the future; I worked and marched, slept, ate, and did what I was ordered; suffered the most awful hardships and bore all kinds of shameful treatment. And during sleepless nights I dreamed of love— love lost forever. . . .

Some five hundred years I wore the uniform of the Legion. So at least it seemed to me.

Then—the great change came. One day there was a letter for me.

Love had found me out across a continent. I read and read and read again.

That was the turning-point of my life. I broke my fetters, and I fought a hard fight for a new career. . . .

Now the jewel happiness is mine.

Erwin Rosen

Hamburg, 1909

CHAPTER 1

Légionnaire!

Another man, feeling as I felt, would have preferred a pistol-bullet as a last resource. I went into the Foreign Legion. . . . It was evening when I arrived in the old fortress of Belfort, with the intention of enlisting for the Legion. Something very like self-derision made me spend the night in the best hotel. Awakening was not pleasant. The sunrays played hide-and-seek upon the lace of the cover, clambered to the ceiling, threw fantastic colours on the white little faces of the *stucco* angels, climbed down again, crowded together in a shining little heap, and gave the icy elegance of the room a warm tone. Sleepily I stared at their play; sleepily I blinked at the enormous bed with its splendid covering of lace, the curious furniture, the wonderful Persian rug. Then I woke up with a start and tried to think. A thousand thoughts, a thousand memories crowded in upon me. Voices spoke to me; a woman's tears, the whispering of love, a mother's sorrow. And some devil was perpetually drumming in even measure: lost, lost, lost forever. . . .

For the second time in my life I felt the Great Fear. An indescribable feeling, as if one had a great lump in one's throat, barring the air from the lungs; as if one never could draw breath again. I had once experienced this fear in the valley of Santiago de Cuba, when one of the first Spanish shells from the blockhouse on San Juan Hill burst a few feet from me. This time it was much worse.

Ah well, one must try to forget!

I dressed with ridiculous care, paid my bill in the "*bureau,*" and earned a lovely smile from *madame* for my gold piece. Ah, *madame,* you would hardly flash your pretty eyes if you knew! The head waiter stood expectant at the door, bending himself almost double in French fashion. He reminded me of a cat in bad humour.

9

I gave him a rather large silver piece.

"Well, my son, you're the last man in this world who gets a tip from me. Too bad, isn't it?"

"*Je ne parle pas. . . .*"

"That's all right," said I.

I walked slowly through the quaint narrow streets and alleys of Belfort. Shop after shop, store after store, and before each and every one of them stood flat tables packed with things for sale, taking up most of the pavement. Here was a chance for a thief, I thought, and laughed, marvelling that in my despair the affairs of the Belfort storekeepers could interest me. Mechanically I looked about and saw a house of wonderful blue; the city fathers of Belfort had built their new market-hall almost wholly of sapphire-blue glass, which scintillated in the rays of the sun, giving an effect such as no painter has as yet been able to reproduce. I felt sorry that a building of such beauty should be condemned to hold prosaic potatoes and green stuff. Vivacious Frenchmen and Frenchwomen hurried by hustling and jostling each other in the crowded streets. . . . Don't hurry about so. Life is certainly not worth the trouble!

Ironical thoughts could not alter matters, nor could even the most wonderful blue help me to forget. I must get it over.

A very young-looking lieutenant came up the street. I spoke to him in my rusty college French:

"Would you please to direct me to the recruiting office of the Foreign Legion?"

The officer touched his *kepi* politely and seemed rather astonished.

"You can come with me, *monsieur*. I am on the way to the offices of the fortress."

We went together.

"You seem to be German?" he said. "I may be able to assist you. I am adjutant to the general commanding the fortress."

"Yes, I am German, and intend to enlist in the Foreign Legion," I said, very, very softly. How terribly hard this first step was! I thought the few words must choke me.

"*Oh, la la . . .*" said the officer, quite confounded.

He took a good look at me. I seemed to puzzle him. Then he chatted (the boy was a splendid specimen of French courtesy) amiably about this and that. Awfully interesting corps, this Foreign Legion. He hoped to be transferred himself to the "Strangers" for a year or two.

Ah, that would be magnificent.

"The Cross of the Legion of Honour can be earned very easily in Southern Algeria. Brilliant careers down there! *Oh, la la! Eh bien, monsieur*—you shall wear the French uniform very soon. Have you anything particular to tell me?"

Again that curious glance.

I answered in the negative.

"Really not?" the lieutenant asked in a very serious tone of voice.

"No, *monsieur*, absolutely nothing. I have been told that for the Foreign Legion physical fitness is the only thing required, and that the recruiting officers cared less than nothing about the past lives of their recruits."

"You're quite right," said the lieutenant; "I asked in your own interest only. If you had special military knowledge, for instance, your way in the Legion could be made very easy for you."

Sometime later I understood what he meant. Now I answered that I had served in the army like all Germans.

Meanwhile we had reached a row of small buildings. Into one of them the lieutenant went with me, up a flight of steep, rather dirty stairs, into a dingy little office. At our entrance a corporal jumped up from his seat and saluted, and the officer spoke to him in a low tone. Then my little lieutenant left and the corporal turned to me.

"Eh, enter *la Légion?*" he said. "*Mais, monsieur,* you are not dressed like a man desiring to gain bread by becoming *légionnaire! Votre nom?*"

I reflected for an instant whether I should give my right name or not. I gave it, however. It did not matter much.

"*Eh, venez avec moi* to the others. The *médecin* major will be here in a minute."

So saying the corporal opened a door and gave me a friendly push. I drew back almost frightened. The atmosphere of the close little room was unspeakable. It was foul with the smell of unwashed humanity, sweat, dirt and old clothes. Long benches stood against the wall and men sat there, candidates for the Foreign Legion, waiting for the medical examination, waiting to know whether their bodies were still worth five *centimes* daily pay. That is what a *légionnaire* gets—five *centimes* a day. One of the men sat there naked, shivering in the chill October air. It needed no doctor's eye to see that he was half starved. His emaciated body told the story clearly enough. Another folded his pants with almost touching care, although they had been patched so

11

often that they were now tired of service and in a state of continuous strike. An enormous tear in an important part had ruined them hopelessly. These pants and that tear had probably settled the question of the wearer's enlisting in the Foreign Legion.

A third man, a strong boy, seemed very much ashamed of having to undress. These poor men considered nudity a vile and ugly thing, because, in their life of poverty and hunger, they had forgotten the laws of cleanliness. They were ashamed, and every move of theirs told it. There, in the corner, one of the men was shoving his shoes furtively as far as possible under the bench, that the holes in them might not be seen, and another made a small bundle of his tattered belongings, thus defying inspection.

A dozen men were there. Some of them were mere boys, with only a shadow of beard on their faces; youths with deep-set hungry eyes and deep lines round their mouths; men with hard, wrinkled features telling the old story of drink very plainly. Nobody dared to talk aloud. Occasional words were spoken in a hushed undertone. The man beside me said softly, the fear of refusal in his eyes:

"I've got varicose veins. D'you think they'll take me . . .?"

My God, the Foreign Legion meant hope for this man—the hope of regular food! The daily five *centimes* were for him wages well worth having!

The atmosphere was loathsome. I stared at this miserable crowd of hopeless men, at their filthy things, at their hungry faces; I felt like a criminal in the dock. My clothes seemed a mockery. . . .

After what seemed an eternity of waiting the officers came in. A fat surgeon, an assistant and my lieutenant. I would have given something to have asked this doctor why in all the world these men could not be given a bath before examination. . . . First the doctor pointed at me. "Undress!"

While I was undressing, the officers kept whispering together, very softly, but I could hear that they were talking about me, and that the lieutenant said something about "*Officier Allemand.*"

I smiled as I listened. It was very funny to be taken for a quondam German officer. I suppose they took me for a deserter; it certainly must have been rather an unusual event to find a well-dressed man enlisting in the Legion.

The well-dressed man felt annoyed at this curiosity, this openly shown pity. It was absolute torture to me. How very ridiculous it all was I fumbled at my watch-chain, trying to take off the little gold sovereign-case in order to open my waistcoat—I fumed at the stares of the officers who should have been gentlemen. . . . The looks of the doctor said plainly:

"Humph, the fellow actually wears fine underclothes!"

Why should they stare at me? Had I not the same right as these other poor devils to go to perdition in my own way? Why should they make it so hard for me in particular? Then I understood how human their curiosity was, and how ridiculous my irritability. The first step was made. I began slowly to understand what it meant to enlist in the Foreign Legion as a last refuge.

I stood there naked before the *médecin* major, who adjusted his eyeglass as if he had a good deal of time to spare, and who took a long look at me. I stared quietly back at him. You may look as long as you wish, I thought, you fat, funny old fellow with a snub nose. You surely aren't going to complain of my physical condition.

"*Bon*," said the doctor.

A clerk wrote something in a book. This finished the ceremony. The doctor did not bother about such trifles as examining the lungs, heart or eyes. He was for simplifying things. *Monsieur le major* decided with a short look in each case, as the other men took their turn. Three men were refused. An old woman could have diagnosed their condition at a glance—they were cases for a hospital, and their doing military service was absolutely out of the question. The man with the varicose veins, however, was at once accepted. *Bon!* I could see how happy he was over his good fortune, and I envied him. The man had hope. . . .

Before a small window in the wall we new recruits waited, half an hour, an hour. At last the window was opened and the corporal put out his head.

"Snedr!" he called.

Nobody answered.

"Snedr!!" he yelled, getting angry.

Still no reply.

Finally the lieutenant appeared beside the corporal, and looked over his list.

"Oh," he said, "the man does not understand. Schneider!"

"Here!" answered one of my new comrades at once.

"Your name is Schneider?" the lieutenant asked

"Yes, sir."

"Very well, in French your name is pronounced Snedr. Remember that!"

"Yes, sir."

"Sign your name here."

The man signed. One after the other the new recruits were called to the little window, and each signed his name, without bothering to look at what he signed. I came last this time. The lieutenant gave me a sheet of hectographed paper, and I glanced quickly over its contents. It was a formal contract for five years' service in the Foreign Legion between the Republic of France and the man who was foolish enough to sign it. There were a great many paragraphs and great stress was laid on the fact that the "enlisting party" had no right upon indemnification in case of sickness or disability, and no claim upon pension until after fifteen years of service.

"Have you any personal papers?" the lieutenant asked me suddenly.

I almost laughed in his face—he was such a picture of curiosity. In my German passport, however, I was described as "editor," and I had a notion that this passport was much too good for an occasion like this. While searching my portfolio for "personal papers" I happened to find the application form of a life insurance company, with my name filled out. I gave this to the lieutenant with a very serious countenance. It was good enough for this. The officer looked at the thing and seemed quite puzzled.

"Oh, that will do," he finally smiled, and gave me the pen to sign.

I signed. And under my name I wrote the date: October 6, 1905.

"The date was unnecessary," said the lieutenant.

"Pardon me," I answered. "I wrote unthinkingly—it's an important date for me."

"By God, you're right," said he.

In single file we were marched to the barracks. One of the French soldiers who met us on the way stopped, and threw up his hands in laughing astonishment:

"Eh!"

And then, making a wry face, he yelled, in a coarse sing-song:

"Nous sommes les légionnaires d'Afrique. . . ."

Half an hour later three new recruits of the Foreign Legion, the recruit Schneider, the recruit Rader and the recruit Rosen, sat in a little room belonging to the quarters of the 31st French Regiment of Line. All three were Germans. Rader opened the conversation.

"My name's Rader. Pretty good name, ain't it, though it isn't my name, of course. I might have called myself von Rader—Baron von Rader—while I was at it, but I ain't proud. What's in a fine name, I say, if you've got nothing to fill your stomach with? No, the suckers may call me Rader. My real name is Müller. Can't use it! Must have some regard for the feelings of my people. . . ."

"I mustn't hurt their delicate feelings," he repeated with a great roar of laughter.

Then a long knife on the table attracted his attention. He took it up, mimicked the pose of a grand tragedian, opened his mouth and swallowed the knife, as if twelve-inch blades were his favourite repast. All at once the knife lay upon the table again, only to vanish in the coat-sleeve of Herr von Rader and appear again rather abruptly out of his left trousers pocket.

"I'm an artist," Herr Rader, *alias* von Rader, *alias* Müller said with a condescending smile. "A good one, too. Strictly first class. Why, these monkeys of Frenchmen don't know nothing about art! Would they appreciate a true artist? Not a bit of it. Boys, since I hopped over the frontier and made long nose at the German cop I left on the other side with a long face, I haven't had much to eat. Remarkably less than was good for my constitution. So Herr von Rader went to the dogs— to the Foreign Legion, I meant to say. What's the difference—if they don't treat me with proper respect, I'll be compelled to leave them again. On French leave! Scoot, skin out, bunk it—see?"

Then Herr von Rader fished a number of mysterious little boxes out of innumerable pockets, inspected them carefully, turned round to mask his artistic preparations, turned to us again—and his wide-opened satyr-mouth emitted a sheet of flame! Little Schneider (he was very young) stared at the phenomenon with startled eyes.

"Grand, ain't it?" said Herr von Rader quietly. "I've a notion that this *coon* isn't going to waste his resources on French Africa. Oh no! Some fine day I'll give the niggers of Central Africa a treat. I'll go partners with some big chief and do the conjuring part of the business. Heap big medicine! There's only one thing worrying me. How about drinking arrangements? Palm-wine, ain't it? Boys, if only they have such a thing as beer and *kümmel* down there!—Say, old fellow (he turned to me) what do you think about this French *absinthe?*"

I mumbled something.

"Awfully weak stuff!" said Herr von Rader sorrowfully. "No d——d good!"

If the comical fellow had known that, with his drollery and his fantastic yarns, he was helping me to battle with my despair, I suppose he would have been very much astonished. . . .

There was a good deal of story-telling: about the hunger and the misery of such *artistes* of the road; about the little tricks and "petty larcenies," by means of which the ever-hungry and ever-thirsty Herr von Rader had managed to eat occasionally, at least, on his wanderings over the roads of many countries; about drinking and things unspeakable. Most of the stories, however, told of hunger only, plain and simple hunger.

Then Schneider's turn came. His story was very simple. A few weeks ago he was wearing the uniform of a German infantry regiment garrisoned at Cologne. He was then a recruit. One Sunday he had gone drinking with some other recruits and together they made a great deal of noise in the "*Wirthshaus*." The patrol came up. As the non-commissioned officer in command put Schneider under arrest, the boy shoved his superior aside, knocked some of the soldiers of the patrol down and took to his heels. When he had slept off the effects of his carouse in a corner, he got frightened and decided on flight. A dealer in second-hand clothes gave him an old civilian suit in exchange for his uniform. As a tramp he wandered till he reached the French frontier, and some other tramps showed him how to get across the frontier line on a dark night. In the strange country hunger came and—

"We always talked about the Legion. All the other Germans on the road wanted to enlist in the Legion. Anyway, I never could have gone home again. My father would have killed me."

"No, he wouldn't," said Her von Rader wisely. "You would have got all sorts of good things. It's all in the Bible. Yes, it is. . . ."

The door opened and a sergeant came in.

"Is the *légionnaire* Rosen here?"

I stood up.

"The lieutenant-colonel wishes to speak to you. Come along to the parade-ground."

". . . Keep your hat on," said the lieutenant-colonel. He spoke pure German. "No, you need not stand at attention. I have heard of you and would like to say a few words to you. I have served in the Foreign Legion as a common soldier. I consider it an honour to have served in this glorious corps. It all depends on yourself: men of talent and intelligence have better chances of promotion in the Legion than in any other regiment in the world. Educated men are valued in the Legion.

16

What was your profession?"

"Journalist . . ." I stuttered. I felt miserable.

The stern grey eyes looked at me searchingly. "Well, I can understand that you do not care to talk about these things. However, I will give you some advice: Volunteer for the First battalion of the Legion. You have a much better chance there for active service. We are fighting a battle for civilisation in Algeria and many a splendid career has been won in the Legion. I wish you good luck!"

He gave me his hand. I believe this officer was a fine soldier and a brave man.

Herr von Rader of the merry mind and the unquenchable thirst slept the easy sleep of light-hearted men; I heard the German deserter groan in his sleep and call for his mother. All night long I lay awake. The events of my life passed before me in mad flight. I was once more a boy at college; I saw my father standing by the dock at Bremerhaven and heard his last goodbye and my mother's crying. . . . Back to America my waking dreams carried me; I saw myself a young cub of a reporter, and remembered in pain the enthusiasm of the profession, my enthusiasm—how proud I was, when for the first time the city editor trusted me with a "big thing," how I chased through San Francisco in cabs, how I interviewed big men and wormed details out of secretive politicians . . . how I loved this work and how sweet success had tasted. Lost, lost forever.

Forget I must—I tried to think of the time in Texas, the life on the Brazos farm, where hundreds of negroes had learned to respect me—after a little shooting and more kindness shown them in their small troubles; I tried to glory in remembrance of hard riding and straight shooting, of a brutal but gloriously free life. Why should I not live a rough life now? I should be on active service in the Legion. Crouching down behind my rifle in the firing-line, waiting for the enemy. I would have a life of excitement, a life of danger. Hurrah for the wild old life! Grant me adventures, Dame Fortune!

But fickle Lady Fortune would not grant even a night's oblivion. During the long night I fought with a wild desire to scream into the darkness the beloved name. . . . I fought with my tears—

17

CHAPTER 2

L'Afrique

Next morning we assembled on the parade-ground. A sergeant distributed silver pieces amongst us, a *franc* for each man, that being the meagre subsistence allowance given us for the long voyage to the Mediterranean. Besides, each man was given a loaf of bread.

Then a corporal marched us to the railway station. The loaf of bread under my arm prompted me to look persistently at the ground. I was afraid of reading in the eyes of the passers-by wonder, surprise, or, worse still, compassion.

The corporal took us to the Marseilles train, gave us his blessing, smoked a cigarette, and waited patiently until the train started. We travelled alone. But France ran no danger of losing her recruits on the way. The fact that we were intended for the Foreign Legion was written on our military ticket in howling big red letters. The conductor watched with great care. He was a Frenchman and a patriot and had his suspicions that these new sons of France might have the perfidy to break faith and leave the train at some place other than Marseilles. He therefore kept a sharp lookout—occupying a good strategic position right in front of our car—whenever the train stopped at stations. The thing would have been impossible, anyway; with that ticket one could never have passed the platform barriers. Said Herr von Rader: "They know all about their business. We are just little flies, don't you see, sonny, and this fine invention of a ticket is the thread wound about our little legs. We're prisoners, brother mine! "

When we left the train at Marseilles, we saw our patriotic conductor run along the platform, signalling excitedly to a sergeant at the gate.

"I've got them! Here they are!" was the meaning of this human semaphore. The conductor was a taxpayer and took good care that

France should receive her dues.

The sergeant and a corporal received us lovingly. The corporal took charge and marched us through the town, while the sergeant trotted along the sidewalk at a respectful distance. Without doubt he had no desire that anyone should connect him with us. He was quite right. We did not look pretty and the night on the train had not enhanced what little beauty we may originally have possessed.

Along the immense water-front of the port of Marseilles we marched; in the midst of a swarming throng of men, amongst a cosmopolitan human machine in full working blast. Past Arabs carrying heavy burdens and fat Levantines lazily strolling about, surrounded by Frenchmen of the south, always gesticulating, ever talking. Ship lay by ship. Elegant steam yachts were moored alongside of unkempt tramp-steamers, whose neglected appearance told of the troubles of money-making on the high seas. There were Levantine barques with funny round sails, whose crews were dressed in flannel shirts of two exclusive colours: a screaming red and a howling blue. Sailing-ships of some hundred different rigs lay there in line, enormous elevators discharged their unceasing flow of grain, and a colossal swivel bridge hung high in the air on her single pillar, seeming to defy all laws of gravitation.

Casks, barrels, boxes, sacks went flying through the air, past our noses, shoved, pushed, thrown, bundled about, propelled by the heavy fists of men who apparently could not work without a tremendous amount of yelling and screaming. Surely the combined noises of fifteen large cities cannot equal the hellish babel of Marseilles' waterfront.

We had to walk more than an hour before we reached the little fort, once the nucleus of Marseilles' harbour defence, whose sole purpose now is that of a gate through which to pass recruits for the colonial armies of France. Fort St. Jean it is called. Over the mediaeval drawbridge of the fort we marched. An enormous oaken door was opened by a couple of sentries. As we entered, a volley of whistles and yells greeted us—the salute for the new *légionnaires* of France. On the time-worn pavement of the courtyard were crowded in a dense mass the soldiers of the African corps who were waiting for the next troopship. *Spahis* and *Zouaves* and *Tirailleurs*, who crowded round us like a swarm of bees.

"*Oh, la la, les bleus pour la Légion!*" (Here are the blues for the Legion.)

"Why are we called blues?" I asked a *Spahi* corporal who happened to stand near me.

"Blues?" he said. "Oh, well, that means recruits. Officially recruits are called '*les jeunes soldats*,' young soldiers, but in the army we say the blues."

"Wonder what it means," I said.

The corporal lit a new cigarette and explained: "The origin of the name is uncertain. My captain told me once that it represented an old army tradition from Napoleonic times. The soldiers of Napoleon wore very stiff cravats to give shape to the high collars of their uniforms. These cravats are said to have been torture. They held the head like a vice, and it took a long time to get used to them. The recruits actually got blue in the face with these cravats round their necks, to the immense amusement of the old soldiers, who made fun of them: Aha, the blues—look at the blues!"

Herr von Rader (in my memory he always figures as "Herr von Rader") gave me a nudge:

"Say, old chap, take a look at the fellows with the colossal pants!"

The *Spahis* were at their *toilette*, arranging their spacious red trousers in picturesque folds. Herr von Rader looked at them with great wonder.

"My soul—what waste! Why, it's astonishing. Out of a single pair of these pants I could make pants for a whole family and have a fine skirt left for my grandmother! "

Then came the *Spahi's* sashes. Two men helped each other at this important part of their toilet. One *Spahi* would fasten the blue sash, seven feet in length, and about half a yard in breadth, to his hip, and turn quickly about while his comrade held the other end, keeping the sash tight and tense until his brother-in-arms was rolled up in it. The *Spahis* seemed to attach great importance to the sit of their sashes, smoothing and; tightening and retightening them with amusing coquetry.

The great gloomy courtyard was one mass of soldiers. From a gallery a non-commissioned officer read off a string of names from a pay-roll, and in squads the soldiers went up the stairs to receive their travelling allowance. We recruits stood in a corner, not knowing what to do or whom to report ourselves to. Finally a corporal exhorted us to go to the devil. We were in the way. It would not be our turn for a long time. We could wait, we should wait, being nasty recruits, blues, *nom de Dieu*. Mumbling further things descriptive of how he despised blues he went off. Then came soldiers, carrying on boards long rows of little tin bowls.

The *Spahis* and *Zouaves* crowded at once round the steaming pots, but Herr von Rader hurled himself in the fray, and captured portions for all of us. It was thus that I made the acquaintance of *la gamelle*, the venerable tin eating bowl of the French army, baptized *la gamelle* centuries ago. I was tasting for the first time the soup of the French army, a mixture of bread and greenstuffs and small pieces of meat. The cooking of this soup was an ancient, time-honoured custom. The musketeers of Louis XIV., of Cardinal Richelieu and Cardinal Mazarin prepared their soup in the very same fashion.

Lounging about the place we came to the canteen of this curious army hotel, and made our way through a labyrinth of wine-casks, which were massed in front of the little door. There was an awful din inside. We sat down at one of the long tables and were served with the French army wine at fifteen *centimes* a bottle. Good wine, too, but it was impossible to enjoy it quietly, the Lord of the Canteen, a fat little man with greedy eyes, being eager for business—second-hand clothes business.

He pestered us unceasingly with his offers and demands. Herr von Rader sold his boots for half a *franc*, after a great deal of haggling, since he wanted the half-*franc* badly, but objected to going barefooted. The owner of the canteen, however (who evidently thought the buying of good boots at half a *franc* a good thing), solved the difficulty. Out of some corner he conjured a pair of shoes such as the French *Zouaves* wear. Although they were in a bad state of dilapidation, Herr von Rader figured out that four bottles of wine could be exchanged for fifty centimes, and the boots changed owners. . . .

Of my possessions, the fat man desired my overcoat. He complimented me on my overcoat. An exceedingly beautiful overcoat—such an overcoat as a poor man like he, the fat man, would be very glad to have. When I entered the Legion I would have to sell it and I would be sure not to get more than two *francs* for it. He would give me four. I never would get as much as that in Algeria, he said. Half an hour he talked to me in the vain endeavour to talk me out of the overcoat. But the "poor man" had a much too prosperous look about him. Moreover, a *Zouave* whispered in my ear that the *cochon* of a canteen-keeper was getting rich by his little "business." So I told him to go to a place which we generally consider hot and disagreeable.

Then the fat man tried it with the others, and made excellent bargains. For a few copper pieces he bought many things, for the twentieth part of their value, boots and coats and pocket-books. The Swiss recruit even sold his trousers. He got five *sous* for them. He got a pair of old French infantry trousers into the bargain since he had to have some sort of compensation for these very necessary garments. The fat man's greedy eyes had a happy light in them and he bought whatever he could lay his hands on.

There was money to be made even out of the poor devils of recruits for the Legion!

I preferred the open air. Leaving the wine and laughter behind me I walked through the fort and climbed up to the bulwarks. The cannon had vanished; where once they had been mounted there grew little tufts of grass on the gravel. I was quiet and lonesome on the old battlements. They commanded a view of the whole of Marseilles. The city and the port were enveloped in a curious yellowish light, the bright yellow of the South. Through a veil of yellow I saw the enormous massive street-blocks of Lower Marseilles, and far away the little villas of the suburbs, their flat roofs reflecting a multitude of colours, with an ever-dominating *leitmotiv* of yellow. The harbour seemed far away and its noises were dimly audible. The ship masts, the elevators, the bridges looked tiny and delicate as the threads of a giant spider's web.

South of my bulwark there was the ocean and peace. Between the walls of St. Jean and the *vis-à-vis*, an ochre-coloured rocky promontory, there was a stretch of deep blue water, of the most beautiful blue in all the world.

Herr von Rader had followed me. He didn't say a word, but sat quietly on the wall swaying to and fro, like a pendulum. From time to time he spat to the whispering waters below. And how pleased he was when he managed to hit a fisherman. But not a word he said.

Little I cared for Herr von Rader and his contempt of the world. What a strange thing this ocean-bound fortress was! The mighty walls now enclosed but an inn. The fort had been turned into an inn in its old days. Its artillery had been sold for old iron long ago. It had ceased to be a fighting machine. It was a resting-place, an hotel for the recruits of France's colonial army to pass a day and a night until the troopship carried them to Africa or French Indo-China or Madagascar. Every day of the year the old fort received new guests—for a day and a night. Many thousands of men had lodged in it. . . .

Fort St. Jean was France's gate for her colonial soldiers. For a few the gate to the Legion of Honour, for the majority the gate to suffering and misery and sickness, to a nameless grave in the hot sands of Africa.

I wondered whither my road would lead me, in what manner I should perish. . . .

The packet boat on which we were transported to Africa had left Marseilles.

Holding my hands to my ears, so that I might not hear a French word or a French sound and be reminded that I was a *légionnaire*, I stood in the bows staring at the wonders of Marseilles. There were a number of little islands wrapped in blue mist, playing hide-and-seek, until the sun appeared. Now the game was over and the veil of mist disappeared. The hills and the houses lay glorious in an ocean of colour. There was a rocky island with an ancient gloomy castle. I knew it to be the prison of Monte Christo, the great adventurer of the elder Dumas, and I felt very much as the imprisoned Count of Monte Christo must have felt.

Marseilles disappeared. Ocean and sun arranged a wonderful play for a poor devil of a *légionnaire*. Far out to sea the sun would try to catch the little waves, throwing floods of brilliant light on pearly cascading water. And then the little waves escaped again, amidst fun and laughter, and ran off to inspect our ship. They struck the ship's sides and seemed very much surprised that they were so solid. They said so plainly enough, making a great deal of noise and fuss about it. But they soon became good-humoured again and told the nicest stories about fairy palaces of the deep and the peace of the ocean. Unthinkingly I had taken my hands down, and heard my new comrades quarrelling amongst themselves. The wine had not been fairly divided.

The spell was broken.

I recognised now well enough that I was standing on one of the lowest steps of the world's ladder, but I had not expected contempt, disdain and rough treatment to touch me so soon. The ship's cook began it.

"*Nix comprends,*" cried the cook. The old packet of the *Compagnie des Messageries Maritimes*, on which we made the voyage across the Mediterranean to Oran, had made a miserable bargain when hiring that cook. The thing was called Jacques. It even answered occasionally to its name if it felt like it. It was malicious, wondrously versed in profanity, addicted to lying, and very filthy.

The first day there was nothing to eat for us until evening. At three o'clock in the afternoon of the second day we were still waiting, very hungry indeed, for our first meal, and I thought it time to have a talk with Mr. Jacques. I told him that our board was paid for and that we wanted something to eat. Quick, too.

The thing answered with a nicely chosen assortment of oaths. He swore like a—well, like a man from Marseilles. He was pleased to inform me that according to his opinion dirty *légionnaires* were expressly made to do a lot of waiting. If he should happen to have spare time on his hands, he might try and get something to eat for us. But he was not quite sure whether or not he would have time!

Now this pleased me. I knew to a nicety how to arrange matters with this thing.

"Well, my son," I said lovingly, "won't you please take a look at these eight comrades of mine? They are Germans and cannot talk French. But they are very good at smashing things. They're quite experts at that sort of thing. See how they are looking at you? I rather think they are going to beat you horribly."

"*Allez donc!*" remarked the cook dubiously. He seemed uneasy.

"They are Prussians. Very likely they'll kill you. I am going to help them at it."

The cook took a look at me and a second look at the "Prussians." He was rather pale and seemed to think that he was up against it. First he cursed volubly, then he dived into his dark hole of a kitchen and fetched out a tin filled with macaroni, a number of loaves of bread, and a bucketful of wine—about a gallon. There were no knives, however, exactly four forks for nine men, and one little drinking-cup.

The other day one of these packets foundered somewhere on the Algerian coast. I sincerely hope it was the packet I crossed on, and that Jacques the cook was drowned. . . .

On the evening of the second day a visitor came to us from the first-class part of the boat. He was a sergeant in the Foreign Legion and ventured among the third-class passengers to have a look at his new recruits. Being a Belgian, he could not talk German with them, and so I had the honour of conversation with him for a couple of hours.

Yes, the Germans made fine soldiers, although they were very thick-headed. Such an obstinate race! It would be best for me if I foregathered with Frenchmen only in the Legion. My French needed cultivating badly, said the sergeant. Then he ordered a bottle of wine and talked about the Legion. Lies, mostly. One of his stories is worth the telling however.

In 1880 a young German enlisted in the Legion. He was an excellent soldier, spoke a brilliant French, and was considered a good fellow. A detachment of the Legion, of which he was a member, was suddenly attacked by Arabs near Saida. The commanding officer, a lieutenant, was severely wounded, and all of the non-commissioned officers killed at the first attack. Now the young German took command and led a furious onslaught on the attacking Arabs, managing to hold out until help came. Shot in the breast he was carried into camp, and the colonel of the regiment gave his own Cross of the Legion of Honour to the dying man. The young German asked the surgeon whether he had a chance of life. The doctor said yes, of course. But, finally, the new Chevalier of the Legion of Honour was told the truth and thereupon demanded a short interview with his commanding officer.

Telegrams went flying between the little desert station and the capital of Germany.... In the evening the *légionnaire* died. A week later a veiled lady appeared in Saida to take the body to the Fatherland. Chevaliers of the Legion of Honour escorted their dead comrade, and the French flag covered the coffin. The young German had been a royal prince of Prussia!

"Do you actually believe this yarn?" I asked the sergeant.

"It's an absolute fact!" said he, very serious and very much offended.

The same story was told me, with slight variations, many times in the Legion. The "royal prince of Prussia" is part and parcel of the unwritten history of the Legion, told from *légionnaire* to *légionnaire*, and I have often wondered how much truth there may be in the legend. Very likely the man of Saida had been a German aristocrat, the black sheep of some good family, and in the course of time and telling the Legion had made him a royal prince of Prussia.

Oran came in sight. Nine recruits promptly lined up on deck, staring with wondering eyes at the land to whose shores destiny had sent them to work and wage war for strangers, for a nation whose language even they did not understand. Sandstone cliffs formed a rugged coast-line. From their heights batteries were firing. The target was pontooned in the sea at a distance of about 5000 yards from the shore. But the columns of water thrown up by the bursting shrapnel never reached it. The old sergeant shrugged his shoulders.

"I am not interested in any shooting but in ours," he said; "anyway, at shooting with the old Lebel gun the Legion can beat any on earth."

He was at least loyal to his Legion, the old grey-haired sergeant, even if he did tell so many lies. . . .

The batteries were at any rate excellently masked. It was quite impossible to detect their positions. Even when the old sergeant showed me where they were mounted, I could see nothing. High up on the crags the heavy cannon had been built in, behind little sandhills, flanked by large rocks, the whole arrangement looking so very much like nature that none could have suspected that it was artificial. The positions of the guns were perfect.

We gained the harbour. Suddenly the cliffs opened out East and West, leaving an enormous gap. Out jumped, as from a conjurer's box, the fortress of Oran, a maze of flat-roofed houses on hilly ground. The inner harbour was ridiculously small, just a little square, its room quite taken up by twelve torpedo-boats, two small cruisers and half a dozen merchant ships. We had hardly touched the pier when a corporal jumped on board. The famous corporal of the French army, the maid-of-all-work, the busy French corporal who attends to everything and has more real work to do than all the officers of a company together. He read off our names from a list and marched us off to quarters.

It was a novel scene that met our gaze. Negroes, sparingly attired in loin-cloth and red *fez*, hurried past in a strange shuffling quickstep, carrying enormous loads on their heads; taciturn Arabs stood around, wrapped from head to foot in white *burnous*-cloth; officers promenaded with their womenfolk and occasionally some fine lady would give us a look of curiosity and compassion. A *Spahi* orderly galloped by on a foaming horse and yelled in high amusement:

"*Bonjour, les bleus!*"

We were marched across the city square. The surroundings and houses had nothing typical about them until we began to pass through little alleys and byways, where naked black children were playing and rolling in the dirt and filth.

Then the sand came. The fine African sand that plays such a *rôle* in a *légionnaire's* life. But the road was an ideal road, hard as stone under its sandy covering. A generation of *légionnaires*, now long dead, had built this road leading to the barracks high up in the hills. The road swept in mighty curves along the cliffs. After an hour of marching we came to some very antiquated barracks. They were a counterpart of Fort St. Jean in Marseilles, one of the military hostelries for the many men needed to feed France's colonial stomach. In the courtyard a lieutenant called the roll and seemed very much amused when the new French soldiers answered to their names with a stentorian German: "*Hier!*"

We were assigned a nasty little hole of a room. A long wooden bench ran along one side. The bare boards, fifteen feet long and six feet broad, were to form our bed. There was a pitcher of water in one corner and a pile of thin brown blankets lay in another. The earthen floor was covered with half-smoked cigarettes and rubbish.

After dark I slipped out, glad indeed to leave the wooden bench. The unventilated little hole was not good enough for a dog! I found a snug, quiet little corner in the courtyard and lay down, wrapped in my overcoat—for about five minutes. Then shadowy figures in the uniform of the Legion paid me a visit.

Yes, a fine evening. Brilliant idea of mine, to sleep in the open air. Filthy place, those quarters for recruits! Yes, *nom d'un petard!* The shadowy figures were old *légionnaires*, on special duty to keep the barracks in order. Did I like the Algerian wine? They wanted to know. I did not know anything about it? Impossible! Did I know that the price of a "litre," of a full quart, was but four *sous* even up here on the hills? Remarkably fine wine!

"It's a pity [described with a variety of choice epithets] that we haven't the [here followed a similar ornate flow of oaths] four *sous*. And the canteen isn't closed yet!"

Small wonder that then I made my first purchase in Africa. Several bottles of wine.

. . . Somebody knocked at a door hard by, attracted by the jingling of bottles presumably. The knocking was quite modest at first. Then it became imperious.

"Who is it?" I asked.

"Oh, that's Reddy. He's thirsty, I suppose," said one of the *légionnaires*. "He's in the lock-up."

My new friends seemed to regard "being in the lock-up" as the most natural thing that could happen to a *légionnaire*. We all went to the door of the cell. There was a small air-hole high up in the wall and presently a hand holding a tin cup appeared.

"Fill up!" a gruff voice demanded.

One of the *légionnaires* climbed on another's shoulders and emptied the contents of half a bottle into the tin cup.

"That's all right!" said the poor prisoner.

"What is he locked up for?" I wanted to know.

This the story.

In the Legion he was nicknamed Reddy, being the happy possessor of a flaming head of red hair. Reddy was a veteran who had ten years of service to his credit and knew well enough that he was no good for anything in all the world except soldiering in the Legion. Ten years is a long time. But, when he was sent to the lonely old barracks on the Oran cliffs to play at housekeeping for recruits, a great desire for liberty came upon him. For hours together he would stare at the ocean. Finally he walked quietly down to the harbour on a fine evening and took his pick amongst the fishermen's boats. He did not waste time in considering whether or not the Arab proprietor of the chosen boat would like his proceedings.

Such things as boats' chains did not worry Reddy. A large stone did the business. Reddy gave the boat a shove, hoisted sail, and sailed joyfully away. Spain was not far, and luck was with the deserter. In exactly seventeen hours the *légionnaire* reached the Spanish coast. He had landed at a very desolate spot, but after hunting about he managed to find fishermen's huts. Presently he was the guest of rough coast Spaniards, who did not quite know what to make of the man in red breeches. He got dried fish and nice clear water to live on. Reddy had forgotten all about civilian life, but in his dreams of freedom dried fish and water had not cut a special figure. He did not like it.

He changed his mind, however, when a pretty Spanish girl appeared. The girl happened to be the wife of the man who had fed Reddy. The *légionnaire* neither knew nor cared. He chatted with the girl for an hour or so in a mixture of French and bits of Spanish and sign-talk, enjoying himself well enough until the husband joined in the conversation with a big knife. A gorgeous fight ensued. The other fishermen assisted their friend and Reddy had a hard run for it. But he reached his boat and got safely away, cursing freedom, Spain, and dried fish. For some time he cruised about and finally decided definitely that freedom was no good. In twenty-five hours he was back in Oran. The Arabian fisherman (who had seen the boat coming and wanted to talk things over) received a series of mighty kicks from Reddy in lieu of payment. Then the disgusted deserter reported to his commanding officer. He explained that he had jumped into the boat just for fun, that a big wind—a horrible storm, sir—had torn the boat from its chain and carried it out to sea. "Yes, sir, I nearly starved. . . ."

The captain happened to be a man with a sense of humour and Reddy got off with twenty days' imprisonment.

"Damned lucky fellow, that! It's a wonder that he was not sent to the penal battalion. That means dying by inches, you know," said the *légionnaires*, and uncorked the last bottle. I stared at them. They laughed about Reddy's luck. They thought his adventure very funny, this tragical adventure of a man who knew how to fight for the freedom he desired and then did not know what to do with liberty when he had gained it. My God, ten years in the Foreign Legion! . . .

CHAPTER 3

Légionnaire Number 17889

A bugle sounded. I was lying on the bare ground in a corner of the courtyard, dozing in that strange borderland between sleeping and waking. The bugle bothered me. The sounds were familiar, but my sleepy brain could not place them. Again and again the calls sounded and half dreaming I searched my memory.

Now I remembered. It was the *réveillé*, the morning call of the American army. No, there could be no mistake—one never forgets the quick nervous air of the American regular's morning call, nor its impressive text:

I can't get 'em up,
I can't get 'em up,
I can't get 'em up in the morning!
I can't get 'em up,
I can't get 'em up,
I can't get 'em up at all!

The old familiar sounds very naturally suggested old remembrances. I dreamt of a misty morning and a hammock slung between two mango-trees, somewhere in the valley of Santiago de Cuba, and a very tired war correspondent listening sleepily to the morning call floating over from the tents of the Sixth Cavalry hard by. A hazy recollection of fantastical foreign legions and broken fortunes crept into the dream. But surely there were no such things. Little Smiley, trumpeter of "B" troop of the Sixth, was sounding the morning call in his funny, drawn-out fashion—of course it was Smiley:

I can't get 'em up at all. . . .

It was but a dream. Awakening, I sat up and stared about me. Where was I anyway? No mango-trees here, no tents, no Sixth Cavalry. And very slowly I realised that Cuba and war corresponding were things of the past, that the pebble-stones of the courtyard were part and parcel of a French barrack and the soldiers in flaming red trousers running about in the courtyard had a perfect right to call me their comrade. There had been no mistake however about the morning call. There it sounded for the third time: "*I can't get 'em up*"—the *réveillé* of the U.S. regulars!

The riddle's solution was rather simple: The "*get 'em up*" signals of the French and the American army are exactly the same.

For three days we stayed at the old barracks high up on the cliffs near Oran. On the third day the packet brought a new batch of recruits for the Foreign Legion, twenty men, most of them Germans. We were all bundled into a rickety little railway train and, at an average speed of about fifteen miles an hour, we raced towards the South, to Sidi-bel-Abbès, the recruiting depot of the Foreign Legion, and headquarters of the Legion's first regiment, the "*Premier Etranger.*"

It took us six hours to reach Sidi-bel-Abbès. As the distance was about eighty miles, I considered this a very poor performance and felt personally aggrieved by the train's slowness. I had yet to learn that from now on time would be no object to me. After leaving Oran our train crawled through beautiful gardens and pretty little *villas*. The gardens were followed by long stretches of fields and farmhouses, and then at last civilisation vanished. The desert sands of Africa claimed their right. The burning sun shone upon wavy lines of endless sandhills, upon naked sand.

After six hours' ride we arrived in Sidi-bel-Abbès. The little station was swarming with men in the uniform of the Foreign Legion. At the primitive little platform gate stood a guard of non-commissioned officers, carefully watching for would-be deserters.

A corporal took charge of us and we fell in line to march to the Legion's barracks.

This first march through the streets and byways of Sidi-bel-Abbès was a strange experience. The city of the Foreign Legion seemed to be composed of peculiar odours and yellow colours in many varieties. I tried to classify the Sidi-bel-Abbès smell, but the attempt was a miserable failure. The strangely sweet scents coming from everywhere and nowhere, which apparently had a very composite composition, defied a white man's nose. They were heavy, dull, oppressive; now reminding one of jasmine blossoms, now of mould and decay. In an atmosphere of yellow floated these scents. The atmosphere was yellow; yellow were the old-fashioned ramparts of Sidi-bel-Abbès, built by soldiers of the Legion many years ago; yellow was the fine sandy dust on the streets; glaring yellow everywhere.

The green gardens on the town's outskirts seemed but animated little spots in a great compact mass of yellow. Far away in the background the colossal ridges of the Thessala mountains towered in gigantic shadows of pale yellow. Even the town's buildings flared up in bright yellow. The people of Sidi-bel-Abbès, adapting themselves to nature in mimicry, must needs paint their houses yellow! There were a few other colours, but the universal yellow swallowed them up without mercy.

Between long rows of stately palms and through shady olive groves we marched. An omnibus rattled past. All the seats were occupied by Arabs. The white splendour of a mosque shone from afar. On the balcony of its high minaret a Mohammedan priest in flowing white robes slowly walked to and fro, sharply outlined against the sky. The mosque was far away, but I could hear the priest's sonorous voice calling to prayer:

"*All' il Allah....* God is God."

We passed through the ancient gates of the city, which was surrounded with thick, clumsy walls, encircling all Sidi-bel-Abbès. The old walls had seen plenty of fighting. In their time they had been very useful to the small garrison in the continuous struggle with the Beni Amer, who had again and again tried to retake the place. Along the large well-kept road we marched. Suddenly, at a turning, the barrack buildings loomed up on both sides of the road—the *Spahis'* cavalry barracks and the quarters of the Foreign Legion.

In single file we marched through a small side entrance alongside of the cumbrous barrack gate. On a long bench near the gate the guard was sitting. They stared at us, grinning stupidly. Their sergeant, with his hands in pockets and a cigarette between the teeth, sized us up, apparently inspecting our physique as if he were taxing a herd of cattle. Then he passed judgment.

"*Pas bon!*" he remarked laconically to the corporal who escorted us. "No good!" An ugly welcome it was. I stared at the immense gravel-covered barrack yard and its scrupulous cleanness, at the immense buildings and their naked fronts, at the bare windows. Why, this must be a madhouse and I—surely I must be a madman, who had to live for five years (five years said the contract) in a place like this. A weird feeling crept over me. I must have lost my way. The moor had caught me. I was lost in the jungle. Shut in by these walls I must spend my life. Must I live among these uniformed human machines, amongst unthinking, unfeeling automatons? My head swam. A feeling of despair came over me. . . .

Everywhere in the barrack buildings windows were thrown open, and *légionnaires* put their heads out, yelling:

"*Eh—les bleus! Bonjour, les bleus!*"

From all sides they came at a run, calling out to each other joyously, "*Les bleus.*" Our arrival appeared to be an amusement that should not be missed. Hundreds of *légionnaires* gathered around us, while we were waiting for orders in front of the regimental offices. The contrast between the snowy neatness of their white fatigue uniforms and our shabby attire was very much in their favour. We stood a crossfire of questions, answers and jokes.

"Hello! Hadn't enough to eat, eh?" somebody yelled in German.

"That's as may be," replied Herr von Rader in cutting sarcasm. "You didn't come to the Legion because you had too much money, did you?" Applause and laughter greeted this answer.

"Any one from Frankfort amongst you?" another asked. "*Merde!*" said he, as nobody replied and turned and walked off.

Then came a surprise. A negro in the uniform of the Legion stalked up to me, regarding me dubiously, shaking his head as if he was not quite sure what to make of me.

"Talk U.S.?" he asked finally.

"Guess I do," I said.

"Golly," yelled the nigger, "here's another! You'se a h— of a d—— fool! *Doucement, doucement*, white man—now, don't get mad. You'se surely is a fool! What in h— you want to come here for?"

The humour of the situation struck me. Besides, I always rather liked darkies.

"What did *you* come here for?" I asked him.

"Me?" said the nigger disgusted, "me? This child's been fooled, see? I'se in Paris (this here nigger's been 'bout pretty much) and a great big doggone Paris cop nabbed me, see? Oh, 'bout miffing particular. I'se been having a swell time in one ob dem little Paris restorangs—sweet times, honey! I'se kissed all the girls and I'se kicked eberyding else. Say—it was a mess. But this here cop got in and he got me all right no flies on the Paris cops, honey! In the station house they done a lot of talking to this here nigger, 'bout French penitentiaries, mostly. They did done tell me, it was penitentiary or Legion. This child stuck to the

American Consul, o' course. Say, he was no good either. Says he, he done got no time to go fooling wid fresh niggers. Take yer medicine, says he. Which I did taking the Legion. *Nix* penitentiary for me. That's what this child come here for, sonny! Bet yer a cigarette you'se be as sick of them Legion people in 'bout four weeks as this nigger is, sure. No good. *Nix* good. D—— bad!"

"I knew that before," said I.

"Then you'se sure done gone crazy, to come he-ar, sonny. Wait a bit, white man. I'se going to tell Smith. He's an American. He's all right. So long!"

And in the shambling gait of his race he walked hurriedly away. One of the recruits hailed from Munich. He was in high debate with another Bavarian *légionnaire*. . . .

"You're from Munich, you fool? There's no beer here!" the old *légionnaire* yelled. "Why didn't you stay in Munich and stick to the beer, eh? Isn't it bad enough if one Munich fool drinks their sticky old wine? Why, I've almost forgotten how a *Masskrug* looks, and what the *Hofbräuhaus* is like. It's a sinful shame, it is. Yes, there's no beer here. You'll be surprised, you will!"

I was still laughing at the two *légionnaires* from the city of beer and "*Steins*" when an old soldier started talking to me very softly.

"Won't you give me your suit of clothes? You must sell it, you know, and you will not get more than a few *sous* for it."

I looked at the man. "Why do you want my clothes?" I asked him.

"To get away! I must get out of this! My God, if I had civilian clothes, I might get through. I'd run away at once and I am pretty sure I could manage to sneak out of Algeria. You'll give me your suit, won't you? This is about my only chance. I'll never have enough money to buy a suit. Is it all right? As soon as you are uniformed, I'll come for the suit. I can easily find out in what company they are going to put you."

Again the man looked at me with scared, pleading eyes, anxiously waiting. He was evidently in deadly earnest. I was deeply impressed. He meant to desert, of course. I had read enough about the Foreign Legion to know that desertion from that corps was a desperate and perilous undertaking. This poor devil was determined to risk it—and I could help him. It occurred to me that, in a very short time, I might feel very much as he felt now. Certainly he should have my clothes.

"You can have them and welcome."

34

"That's the best piece of luck I've had since I came to this '*ver-damnte*' Legion," said the man. He was a German, a Pomeranian, I should say, judging from the dialect he spoke.

Meanwhile Black (John William Black was the negro's very appropriate name) had come back, with a bugler who looked as much like a "Yank" as anybody could look.

"So you're American?" the bugler asked.

"About half of me is," I said.

"Oh, German-American! I see. That's all right. It's pretty tough work here in the Legion; well, you'll see for yourself. I'm mighty glad to talk U.S. to a white man. The nigger's no good—you know you're not, Blacky!—and me and him are the only two Americans in this damfool outfit. Blacky's always kicking up a row about something, and he spends most of his time in prison, and when he's not there he generally manages to get drunk. Beat's me, on what! He's a pretty hard case, ain't you, Blacky?"

"Shoore—I—am, you son-of-an-old-trumpet!" grinned the negro.

"I wonder what company you'll be assigned to," continued the "son-of-an-old-trumpet." "If the sergeant should ask you whether you had any preference, tell him you would like to be assigned to the eleventh. That's my company. We could play poker. I could show you the ropes, too. Life's no snap in this outfit, you know!"

"Aren't there any other Americans in the Legion?"

"Oh yes, about twenty. There are seven with the fourth battalion of the first, somewhere in Indo-China. The second regiment of the Legion in Saida has thirteen or fourteen American *légionnaires*. Two of them are sergeants, and one is colour-sergeant; McAllister is his name. He's a good man. Yes, about twenty boys from the States have a hand in this Legion business!"

"*Garde à vous!*" commanded the sergeant, coming out of the regimental offices. "Attention!"

The roll was called and we were divided up amongst two companies, the third and the eleventh. I was assigned to the eleventh—"*la onzième*." We marched across the drill-ground to one of the barrack buildings. In the storeroom of the eleventh company underwear and white fatigue uniforms, woven from African "*Alfa*" fibres, were issued to us. Then each man got a nightcap. These rather unsoldierly caps were worn by all of the *légionnaires* in the cold African nights. Soap and towels the sergeant-major also distributed, remarking that we seemed to be badly in need of soap, which certainly was true. We were then marched off to a small house at the back of the drill-ground. Its one room contained a number of primitive shower-baths. While we were bathing, a sergeant watched at the door, critically inspecting and exhorting us again and again:

"*Bon Dieu*, get a good wash! Be sure you get a thorough wash!"

After we had dressed in the fatigue uniforms he commanded: "Take your civilian clothes under your arms," and led us to a little side entrance of the barracks. A sentinel opened the door—and hell broke loose. Arabs, Levantines, Spanish Jews, niggers beleaguered the door, and the sentinel had to use the butt of his rifle—he seemed to like the job though—to keep them from getting in. In many languages they yelled, gesticulating with hands and feet, jumping about, making a horrible noise. At first I had no idea what it all meant. Then I understood. They wanted to buy our clothes . . . that was all. They got very excited over the business and seemed to think they could buy our things for a copper piece or two. Finally the sergeant acted himself as our agent and arranged prices.

Even then it was a good thing for them. Any second-hand clothes dealer in any of the world's large cities would have looked at the scene with the blackest envy. A good suit of clothes fetched two *francs*, boots eighty *centimes*, white shirts and cravats were thrown into the bargain. Every one of the native "men of business" knew well, of course, that the recruits were forced to sell at once. Civilian clothes are not allowed to be kept in the Legion. None of the recruits got more than three or four *francs* for his things. It was a great piece of swindling. I was saved the trouble of bartering with the native riff-raff. The *légionnaire* who took an interest in my clothes turned up, while the sergeant was busy at the door, pulled my clothes-bundle softly from under my arm, stuffed it under his jacket and walked away in a hurry. Next day he was missed, Smith told me. . . .

Our next visit was to the eleventh company's office, where our names and professions were entered on the company's lists. It was nothing but a matter of form. Herr von Rader declared that his father was the Chancellor of the German Supreme Court and that he himself was by profession a juggler and lance-corporal of marine reserves. And the colour-sergeant put it all down in the big book without the ghost of a smile.

Each of us was given a number, the "*matricule*" number of the Foreign Legion. Our names mattered nothing. We were called by numbers: My number was 17889.

From now on I was merely a number, a strict impersonal number. . . . They number men in penitentiaries. It was just the same in the Legion. I had got what I wanted. The great Legion's impersonality had swallowed me up. What was my name now? . . . Number 17889. . . .

CHAPTER 4

The Foreign Legion's Barracks

The eleventh company's storeroom was in a state of siege. We besieged the place, pushing and being pushed, hunting for standing room, but everywhere standing in somebody's way. The "non-coms" had very soon exhausted their vocabulary of strong language and could only express their feelings in fervent prayers that fifteen thousand devils might fly away with those thrice confounded recruits—*ces malheureux bleus*. A corporal, two sergeants, a sergeant-major and half a dozen *légionnaires* detached for storeroom work continually fell over each other in their haste to get done at last with the trying on of uniforms and with the issue of the kit.

Countless jackets and pants were tried on; they put numerous *kepis* upon our sinful heads, and again and again they anathematised our awkwardness in priceless adjectives. In big heaps the property of our future Legion life was dealt out to us; red pants and fatigue uniforms, blue jackets and overcoats, sashes, knapsacks, field-flasks, leather straps and belts, a soldier's kit in a bewildering jumble.

"Ready!" said the sergeant-major at last with a grin of relief. "And that's something to be thankful for. Here, Corporal Wassermann, take them away. *Voila!* Off with your mess of recruits. Try and make *légionnaires* out of the beggars. Yes, you'll find it a big contract. I wish you joy, Corporal Wassermann."

"*En avant, marche*" commanded the corporal. Once more the non-commissioned officers of the storeroom told us exactly what they thought of us and where they wished us to go. Their remarks were extremely pointed and expressive of their disgust.

We mounted three flights of stairs and the passing *légionnaires* of the company stared at us in curiosity.

Through a long corridor we marched, until the corporal kicked a door open and led us into a big room, our future quarters. We looked about our new home. Twenty beds were in the room, ten on one side, ten on the other, perfectly aligned. In the middle of the room stood two big wooden tables and long benches, scoured gleaming white. Everything in the place was scrupulously neat and clean. A rack in the corner held our rifles. Suspended from the ceiling, over the tables, there was a cupboard—the "pantry" of our quarters. It struck me as very practical. Knives and forks, the men's tin plates and tin cups, our bread rations were kept there. Half a dozen *légionnaires* were sitting on bunks and benches, cleaning their rifles and polishing their leather belts—our comrades.

Corporal Wassermann, lying in his bunk puffing a cigarette, took a good long look at us. He was little more than a boy.

"*Eh bien,*" he said, "I am your corporal. You will have to learn French as quickly as possible. That's very important. Keep your ears open and listen to everything that's said. That is the right way to go about it. We shall begin drilling tomorrow. Today you will have to arrange your bunks and things. I shall arrange your bunks in such a fashion that each of you shall be placed between two old *légionnaires*. You've only got to watch how they fix their things and do the same. It is all very simple. When you have finished arranging your stuff, you can do what you please."

Then he assigned a bunk to each of us and went off whistling. To the canteen, of course.

"Hallo!" said Smith. He had just come in. "That's all right. So you've not only been sent to the eleventh, but to my room as well. And that's all right. That's my bunk over there at the window. Take the one next. It's been given to a recruit already, you say? Oh, kick him out, kick him out. What do you suppose the corporal cares where you bunk. I'll fix it with him. And that's all right. I'm going to call you Dutchy. Now don't object, because I'm going to call you Dutchy anyhow, see?"

He was evidently pleased. So was I. From the start I had taken a liking to this man with the sharply cut features and the curious air of infinite knowledge. The pasteboard card on his bed said:

Jonathan Smith, N 10247, *soldat 1ère* [1] *classe.*

He was the company's bugler, and had nine years' service in the

---

1. The Foreign Legion and the French army in general make a distinction between first-class privates and second-class privates. The first-class private has the grade of a lance-corporal.

Foreign Legion to his credit. Fever and privation and vice had engraved hard lines in his face, and when he rolled his cigarettes in French fashion, his hands trembled just a little. His hair was quite grey. He had fought against Chinese pirates in French Indo-China, he had campaigned in Madagascar and won the French medal for bravery on colonial service. During this campaign he had been shot in the shoulder and had had a severe attack of jungle fever.

There was no garrison in Algeria, be it on the Morocco frontier, be it on the Sahara line, where he had not been stationed once at least. He was a perfect encyclopaedia of all things connected with the Legion. He could swear fluently in English, German, French, and Arabian, and had even acquired a pretty fair knowledge of Chinese expressions of disgust. He was friend and brother to several Arabs with doubtful characters, he could recite whole chapters of the *Koran* by heart, and knew a great deal about Morocco. Which will be seen later on.

He was in fact a man well worth knowing.

From the very beginning there was a perfect understanding between us. He volunteered the information that he was a native of California and had "seen a few things in his life." I answered with the bare statement that I was a German, and had lived in the United States for some years. Both remarks were the basis for a tacit agreement to keep within the limits of strict impersonality.

He lay on his bunk, and I tried to get some order in my newly issued belongings.

"Your shoulders have been drilled into shape somewhere?" said Smith.

"They were."

"States?"

"No, Germany."

"Oh, I see. Thought you might have been in the U.S. army. Wish I had stuck to it."

"Have you tried the Legion's tobacco yet?" he continued.

We rolled ourselves cigarettes from strong, black Algerian tobacco, and Smith stretched himself comfortably on his bunk with his knees drawn up, his cap pulled down over his eyes. Smoking contentedly, the old soldier preached me the Legion's wisdom:

"There's no money here—the pay is not worth speaking of, I mean. There's a lot of work. It's a hard life all round. That's the Foreign Legion. There's no earthly reason why any man should be fool enough to serve in this outfit, unless he's specially fond of being underfed and overworked. When I come to think of it—I don't know what the dickens made me stay nine years! Because there's something doing once in a while, I suppose. Well, I'll stick it out for the pension now. Anyway, you've joined the Legion—more fool you—you're here and you can make up your mind that you are here to stay. And you must look at things in the right way. Legion life can be stood right enough, if you don't let yourself be worried by anything at all, if you're as ice-cold as Chicago in January, and if you're lucky enough to see something doing.

"Whether we march against the Arabs or Chinese (there's a battalion of us in Indo-China, you know) or to 'Maroc' at last, that's all the same, but it's good to be on the move in the Legion. Then a *légionnaire's* life ain't half bad. Don't ever forget, though, to have your feelings frozen into an iceblock. Don't let anything bother you. No use getting mad about things here. Just say to yourself: '*C'est la Légion.*' When you're dead played out, and you think you can't stand it any longer; when the fever's got you by the neck; when you're sitting and fuming in the *cellule* (that's the prison, Dutchy), or when some sergeant's giving you hell—grin, sonny, and say to yourself: '*C'est la Légion!*' That's the Legion. Do your work and don't worry. If any of the fellows get fresh, hit quick and hit hard—*c'est la Légion.* And don't forget that the main thing in this Foreign Legion business is neatness and cleanliness. You want to have your things in order, you want to be neat. So!"

He rummaged in the bundle of uniform things on my bed, pulling out one by one jackets, pants, shirts, &c., and folding them with astonishing quickness. I watched him in wonder. This old soldier with his big rough hands had fingers as clever as any chambermaid's. Piece after piece he folded rapidly, smoothing every crease with almost ridiculous care. Each of the folded pieces he measured, giving each the same length, from the tips of his fingers to his elbow. Finally he erected with these bundles, upon the shelf at the wall over my bed, an ingenious structure of uniforms, the *paquetage* of the Legion. The *légionnaire* has no clothes-chest like the American regular. To get over this difficulty he invented his "*paquetage,*" which is a work of art, solving the military problem of how to stow away several uniforms in a compact space without crumpling them.

With half-shut eyes the bugler stood in front of my bunk and regarded his handiwork.

"And that's all right," he said. "That's a *paquetage,* how it should be.

It's *fantasie*, pure *fantasie*,'Dutchy dear. Making *fantasie*[2] it is called in the Legion, if one tries to be always *tres chic* and *parfaitement propre*, to be a swell. Yes, that's the Legion. We are lazy by preference, but we're always neat. Always!"

The *paquetage* was not the only miracle. I was very much impressed by the way every bit of available space was put to the utmost use. A *légionnaire* keeps his linen in his haversack. For his letters, his books, for the few other articles of private property he possesses, he finds room in his knapsack; his brushes and his polishing-rags are carefully stored away in a little sack which hangs on the wall. Even the most trivial of his belongings has its appointed place. A *légionnaire* keeps his kit in such perfect order that he can find everything in the dark.

While I was making my bed, the bugler looked on for a while, grinning all the time. Finally he couldn't stand it any longer. He pulled the blankets and the sheets I had spread out away again and started showing me how to make a bed "*à la Legion.*" Bed-making was another of the Legion's tricks. In a few seconds Smith had arranged the bed-clothes in wonderful accuracy, blankets drawn tight as a drum, pillows placed in mathematical exactness.

"*Merde!*" he said, "that's how we *légionnaires* fix our bunks. It's easy enough."

"*Merde?*" I asked, "what does *merde* mean, anyway?"

It was a French word unknown to me. Smith used it continually, underlining his remarks with it, so to speak. He seemed to like it. He pronounced it with much care, lovingly. Naturally I thought that it must be some especially forceful invective, the more so as the sergeant-major in the storeroom (who certainly had not been in good humour) had said "*merde*" about five hundred times in ten minutes. And the other *légionnaires* in the room liked it apparently no less. The "*merdes*" were always flying about. . . .

"Well, what is this *merde*?"

Smith nearly had a fit.

"*Merde?*" he yelled, laughing as if he had suddenly gone crazy, "what *merde* means? Why, you owl, *merde* is ———."

He used a word which certainly does not exist in the vocabulary of polite society, an old Anglo-Saxon substantive, describing a most natural function and expressing huge disgust when used as an invective.

This little word is the favourite substantive of the Foreign Legion.

---

2. This curious expression of the Foreign Legion is, of course, an imitation of the Moorish *fantasia*.

It is *the* substantive of the Legion! The English Tommy rejoices in his time-honoured adjective "bloody," the American revels in his precious "damned," the Mexican cavalryman enjoys his malignant hissing "*caracho*," and the *légionnaire* is distinctly unhappy without his well-beloved "*merde*." It's the most used word in the Foreign Legion. It has suffered curious derivations: *Merdant, merdable*. . . . It has a happy home in all French regiments—it is part and parcel of the French army's soldier-talk. The Legion worships it. Out of it the *légionnaire* has even fabricated a verb. When an officer gives him a "dressing down," the *légionnaire* says simply and devoutly:

"*Il m'emmerde!*"

The French army's primitive substantive of disgust is very ancient. It is time-honoured, it is classical.

At Waterloo the commander of Napoleon's Old Guard is said to have replied to the challenge to surrender, pompously: "The Old Guard dies, but it does not surrender!" In the French army, however, it is an old tradition that he simply yelled:

"*Merde!*"

Invectives of all descriptions were used with much vigour in our quarters just now. The old *légionnaires* took a delight in kicking the clumsy recruits about. In drastic terms they told them exactly what they thought of them, of their past, of their families, of their future. They felt very sorry (so they said) for the poor old eleventh company having been *buncoed* into taking such an awful pack of useless recruits. Many were the fools they had seen in the Legion, but never such idiots as we were. Pretty fellows, those recruits! A nice assortment of pigs! Fine times they (the poor old *légionnaires*) would have, living in the same quarters with these "*bleus*."

"Why—there's one of 'em sitting on my bed. What's this bow-legged monkey doing on my bunk? Get off! Get off quick, son of a jackal! Do you suppose that my bunk's a manoeuvring-ground for dirty recruits? "

The old *légionnaires* knew their business, however.

Abuse alone was not good enough. They wanted to see practical results. So they explained to the *bleus* that recruits, and especially such recruits as now present, could never manage to build a *paquetage* without help. That was a foregone conclusion. Said one of them:

"Can't you see that? If such a thing as intelligence had a place in your empty heads, you would have seen long ago that you needed help. Who's going to help you? We are. We old *légionnaires* will help you—we who know everything and can fix anything. But we're thirsty, you see. *Tant de soif!* Such a thirst. I put it to you: Is it right that recruits, recruits, mind you, who have just sold their clothes and got a lot of money in their pockets, should look on and say nothing, while their betters are dying of thirst. Is it right, eh?"

There the others joined in: "*Allons donc pour un litre*—let's drink a litre in the canteen."

The arguments of the old fellows met with enormous success. At frequent intervals old and young *légionnaires* left the quarters to pay a visit to the canteen and render homage to the immortal "litre" of the Foreign Legion. The whole performance was an old custom. Old *légionnaires* always rejoice when new recruits arrive—anticipating many pleasant walks to the canteen. . . .

One of the recruits, a Swiss, on returning from the canteen found that the greater part of the kit on his bed had disappeared. Almost everything was gone. A complete uniform, a fatigue suit, an over-coat and several other things were missing. The Swiss, scared to death, asked every man in the room if he had seen his things. But his kit had vanished.

The old *légionnaires* gathered about his bunk. Very likely he had lost part of his outfit while coming up the stairs, they said. They told him that one must look after one's kit in the Legion. If he could not find the missing uniforms, he would be certain to be sent to prison at the very least. He might even be punished with deportation into the penal battalion. Losing part of the uniform was the very worst crime known in the Legion.

The Swiss ran up and down the stairs hunting for his lost uniforms, but naturally found nothing.

Again the old *légionnaires* talked to him. They played their part very well.

"You're a poor devil," they said. "We're sorry for you. We'll try and help you. It's a very difficult case, but we might be able to do something. The non-commissioned officer of the third company's storeroom is a pretty decent fellow. He'll do something for an old *légionnaire*. We'll try him. There's just the chance that he will give us the stuff you have lost from his stock of uniforms—for a little money. He's fond of making something on the quiet. Five *francs* would do, and what are measly five *francs* anyway, if they are the means of saving you from prison?"

The poor devil was glad enough to get off with paying five *francs*.

It was just what he had got for his clothes.

. . . Very soon the old soldiers came back. That good fellow of a sergeant had given them everything needed! Faultless new uniforms! And the Swiss recruit thanked the old thieves profusely.

Personally I was angry at the shabby trick played on the poor devil. I had known from the very outset that it was only a trick. The rascals had stolen the recruit's uniforms, and had then sold him back his own things! It certainly was no business of mine, and I did not interfere. In a way the comic side of the thing appealed to my sense of humour, but it was a nasty trick all the same. While I was wondering whether I should tell that fool of a Swiss how he had been done, one of the old *légionnaires* happened to sit down on my bunk.

"Get off my bed!" I said.

Blank astonishment was written on the man's face.

"What d——d cheek for a raw recruit. You impertinent . . ."

"My bed's my bed. Get off. Sit on your own bed. Just now you raised a row because one of us was sitting on yours. Get away from here and be quick about it."

The old *légionnaire* rose slowly.

"*Viens la bas!*" he yelled. "Come down below to the yard with me. I'll teach you that a good-for-nothing recruit should respect an old soldier. Come down!"

Together we descended the stairs, a few other *légionnaires* following. The bugler was amongst them.

"Give him hell," he said. "Look out for his feet! "

I was very pleased with myself. It was bad enough to be in the Legion, but one could at least play the man. . . .

At the back entrance of the company's quarters, in a small alleyway, we found a quiet spot to settle our little difference. He kicked furiously in French fashion, and I barely managed to escape. Then we closed in and in a second were rolling over and over on the gravel-covered ground. Now one had the upper hand, now the other. My antagonist's strength surpassed mine by far. I could do but very little in his iron grip. I began to wonder how many of my ribs would survive the fray. But all at once I got the upper hand.

Again and again he tried to get a grip of my throat, but I caught his hand every time. We rolled over and over. My strength was fast sinking. At the last moment almost, I noticed a big stone on the ground quite near his head. I wrested my hand free. Seizing my antagonist by the hair, I pounded his head against the stone as hard as I could. Once—

twice—four times. . . . His grip relaxed. . . .

"*Assez!*" he yelled, "enough."

"*Très bien*," the onlooking old *légionnaires* said, "very good."

The bugler was disgusted. (So was I.) "Now that's the Legion all over. I wonder why the people here can't box like Christians instead of rolling about like pigs. You've licked him, though. And that's all right."

The man I had "fought" with rose with some difficulty and walked up to me. We shook hands. . . .

"You were in the right when you ordered me off your bed," he said. "*Parbleu*, that was a good idea with the stone. Eh, you'll be a good *légionnaire* very soon. We men of the Legion quarrel often, but at heart we're always comrades. *C'est la Légion!* I propose we return to our quarters again. . . ."

And in the room we brushed the dust from each other's uniforms, like old friends. . . .

"You're tired, I guess," said the bugler with a grin. "Let's go and have a litre."

I had no objection.

"I am paying for this," he declared, as we crossed the drill-ground.

The regimental canteen was in a small building in a corner of the barrack square. We opened the door and—I at least must have looked very much surprised. There was an awful noise in the little room. A great many soldiers were talking and laughing and singing and yelling in many languages; in German, French, English, Italian and Spanish—there was the jingle of many bottles and glasses. As we entered a German was singing:

Trinken wir noch ein Tröpfchen
Aus dem kleinen Henkeltöpfchen,
Oh, Suss . . . a . . . na!

In sharp marching rhythm a Frenchman sang the refrain of one of the Legion's songs:

Le sac, ma foi, toujours au dos . . .

The canteen was crowded. Hundreds of *légionnaires* in white fatigue uniforms or in blue jackets sat on the long benches, drinking, laughing. On the wooden tables bottles stood in long rows and deep red wine sparkled in the glasses.

"There's no room here," I said.

Smith grinned in answer: "Room? *Nom d'un pétard*, what do we

46

want room for? The litre is the main thing, sonny!"

Pushing through the crowd he reached the bar and held up a forefinger with a serious face. This seemed to be a well-known signal to the young woman behind the bar. Without saying a word she took three copper pieces from the bugler, giving him in exchange a full bottle of wine and two glasses. *"Madame la Cantinière"* could not be over twenty years old. Like a queen seated on her throne she held sway behind her bar and ruled the crowd of noisy, yelling *légionnaires* in quiet authority, imposing and comical at the same time.

Madame la Cantinière was the sutler of the Foreign Legion. Old tradition demands that a woman should keep the Legion's canteen. *"Madame la Cantinière de la Legion"* usually is married, but she is the official head of the canteen and not her husband. The business belongs to her. On the march and in the field she wears the blue sutler's uniform and follows the regiment with her little sutler's waggon.

On a bench in the corner Smith found seats for us, and had two big glasses filled (the Legion does not waste time drinking out of small wineglasses!)—had the glasses filled before we sat down.

"Here's luck," he said. "There's no such thing as luck in this place, but one keeps on wishing for it just the same. Here's luck, Dutchy!"

He emptied his glass at a gulp, wiping his soft fair moustache in great satisfaction. *And* he refilled his glass at once.

"The wine's good. And that's all right. Sonny, there are miles and miles of vineyards round this here Sidi-bel-Abbès. The hilly ground near the Thessala mountains is a single large vineyard. There are times in Algeria when they let the wine run on the street. It's so plentiful and cheap that it isn't worth the casks. There would be no Legion, I tell you, if it wasn't for the cheap wine!"

With wondering eyes I surveyed the men in the canteen and the canteen itself. The smoke of many hundreds of cigarettes filled the place with a heavy bluish vapour. The noise was indescribable. One had to yell to be understood by one's neighbour, a quietly spoken word would have been lost in the turmoil. Everybody was yelling and everybody seemed to be in high glee. The *légionnaires* were having what they considered a good time. They jumped on the tables, kicking and dancing, jingled their glasses, threw empty bottles about and made fun of everybody and everything. Every minute the uproar increased. These hard-faced, hard-eyed men were like children at some forbidden game, trying to get as much fun as possible while the teacher was away.

Suddenly a man with a wonderfully clear and strong voice began singing a love-song. Noise and tumult ceased at once. I listened in amazement. A *légionnaire* sang for his comrades, in a beautiful tenor voice, in a voice reminding me of great singers I had heard long ago. A poor devil of a *légionnaire* possessed a voice many a singer would have envied. He sang a French song, every verse closing pitifully:

L'amour m'a rendu fou. . . .

The song of a lover who had loved and lost, a song of love and ladies, of love's delights and love's misery, sung in the canteen of the Foreign Legion.

With burning eyes I looked at the listening throng of men in red and blue until I saw nothing but their shadowy outlines like a far-away *fata Morgana*—I was lost in a dream of memories.

Absolute quiet reigned. The song held these men of rough life and rougher manners spellbound; the glorious mellow voice, now clear as a trumpet, now low and sweet as a woman's caress, must have appealed to every heart. The song was at an end:

L'amour m'a rendu fou. . . .

For a moment, for a few seconds, all remained hushed. And then one would think that these men were ashamed of having been so soft-hearted. A *légionnaire* jumped on a table and yelled:

"Silence. . . . No more fool songs for us! *Vive le litre!*"

"*Le litre!*". . . a hundred men roared. The shouting and the uproar and the noise commenced anew. Blacky, the negro, had come in and was soon dancing the dance of his race. He was a master of the turnings and twistings of the cake-walk. There were universal yells of appreciation as he bent backwards, high-stepping grotesquely. Blacky was much applauded and seemed to be a very happy nigger. *Madame la Cantinière* did a roaring trade. The copper pieces were continually jingling on the tin-covered surface of the bar. *La Cantinière* was a very busy woman this evening, passing many hundreds of wine bottles to her thirsty *clientele* of *légionnaires*. Glasses were broken, pieces of glass lay everywhere on the tables and on the floor, and here and there little red pools of wine had formed. The fun grew fast and furious and the noise almost unbearable.

My friend the bugler had emptied glass after glass and was in high good humour.

"Why, it is the regiment's holiday!" he laughed.

The "fifth day" it was—payday. The Legion's humour called payday the regimental holiday. This humour was somewhat grim in view of the fact that pay in the Legion meant but five *centimes* a day, twenty-five *centimes* for the pay-roll period of five days. Twenty-five *centimes* are almost exactly five cents in American, or twopence-half-penny in English money.

So the Legion's "holiday" was at the bottom of all the noise and fun in the canteen! These men in the Legion measured the passing of time by their miserable paydays only. Such a fifth day marked the glorious epoch when two comrades could buy exactly five "*litres*" of wine for their joint pay. Certainly such frivolity punished itself: there was no money left for the next five days' tobacco. So wise men in the Legion buy the customary package of tobacco for three *sous*, and drink but one bottle of wine every five days. This is what the soldier of the Foreign Legion works for: One bottle of wine and one package of tobacco every five days!

Shrilly a signal sounded through the noise:—lights out! *Madame la Cantinière* held up her hand, made a funny little bow, and said with a smile:

"*Bonsoir, messieurs.*—Goodnight, gentlemen."

The Legion teaches obedience. . . . In a very few seconds the canteen was empty and everybody was hurrying across the drill-ground to quarters.

When roll-call had been finished in our quarters and everybody had gone to bed, I quietly left the room. Sleep did not appeal to me that night. The still of night lay over the barrack-yard. The white moonlight shone on the bare walls of the barracks. The stars of far south glittered in their trembling beauty. I stared up into the splendour of the heavens and brooded over happiness far away—passed—dead, . . .

I heard footsteps and saw a shadow moving somewhere on the other side. And over there a trembling awkward voice sang softly:

L'amour m'a rendu fou. . . .

Far into the night I crouched in a corner of the Legion's barrack-yard.

The first days, the first weeks of life in the Legion were quite sufficient to render me immune against strange things and strange sights. Sometimes it seemed to me as if my nerves were quite dulled. Every day brought monstrous sights and hideous impressions. I shuddered at unheard-of things and wondered at these strange specimens of humanity. But the next moment some new horror made me forget what I had just seen.

In a few minutes' walk with the bugler round the barrack-yard one could meet with a variety of sights like the following:

A *légionnaire* ran past us, shrieking in extreme pain, splashed with blood. He had cut off the forefinger and middle finger of his right hand so as to be unfit for active service.

A poor crippled Arab, bent with age, stopped when he saw us. He was evidently on his way to the kitchen buildings to beg for food. In his hands he carried a Standard oil-can. A Standard oil-tin as receptacle for food in connection with an Arab, Algeria and the Foreign Legion struck me as something distinctly new. But there was more to follow. In very broken German the Arab addressed us:

"*Gut' Tag, légionnaires. Cigarette! Ick sein deutsch—Magdeburg gewesen—1870.*"

The man had fought in the great Franco-German war and had been in Magdeburg as a prisoner of war!

Hardly had I recovered from my surprise when a passing *légionnaire* made me stare in horror. The man had the grinning image of a skull tattooed on his forehead! He smiled at my frightened face and was evidently very pleased at the impression he had made. I remember saying to the bugler how horrible it was that a man should disfigure his face for life in such a manner, and I remember that Smith only shrugged his shoulders in reply.

"Why, that's nothing," he said. "Tattooing of that kind is quite customary in the Battalion of the Disciplined."

I could not agree with the bugler, I could not see a mere freak in this horrible tattoo-mark. To me it spoke of hope lost forever, of a life so dreadful that a man no longer cared whether he was disfigured or not.

Pleased with the notice he attracted, the *légionnaire* with the skull on his forehead walked up to us and spoke to me:

"Eh, recruit, do you want to see something that very old *légionnaires* only have got?"

He showed me a tobacco-pouch, apparently made of fine soft leather:

"This is made of the breast of an Arab woman," said the man of the skull. "It is a very good tobacco-pouch. Made it myself. There are only seven in the whole regiment now. Chose—*n'est-ce pas?* That is something worth seeing!"

With a grin of vanity he walked away.

"Tobacco-pouch—an Arab woman's breast—my God, what is the meaning of this?" I asked of the bugler.

Smith told me all about those horrible pouches. The man of the skull had not lied. During the last insurrection of Arabs in Algeria, in grim warfare far in the South, Arabian women had horribly mutilated the bodies of *légionnaires* and inflicted horrible tortures on the wounded. The soldiers of the Legion, maddened, thirsting for revenge, gave quarter to no Arab woman during those times. They retaliated in kind. . . . Of the horrible deeds they committed the dreadful tobacco-pouches gave evidence.

On the same day I witnessed for the first time the prisoners' march of punishment. I stood aghast.

Behind the quarters of the fourth company, in a small square between barrack building and wall, about thirty men were marching in a continuous circle, to the sharp commands of a corporal:

"*À droit—droit; à droit—droit*; right about, march; right about, march."

The prisoners marched round their narrow circle in fast quickstep, almost at a run, with backs deeply bent. Their knapsacks were filled with sand and stones, every man carrying a burden of from seventy to eighty pounds. All the prisoners had a hard strained look on their faces. Their fatigue uniforms were torn and soiled. Guards with fixed bayonets stood at the corners of the square, guarding the marching prisoners.

The term prisoner must not be misunderstood. These men were not criminals. The *légionnaires* marching in the "*peloton des hommes punis*" had been punished with a term of imprisonment for small offences in the matters of discipline. They were not only put into prison, but also had to march on their ridiculous march of punishment for three hours every day, the stones in their knapsacks causing bad sores on their backs. These men, punished for some paltry military offence, were certainly treated as if they were criminals of the worst description.

I tried to imagine what I should feel and what I should do if a sandsack were put on my back and I were driven round in this maddening march. . . . It was dangerous to think of these things.

"*Allez*, let's go," said the bugler. "We all go to prison some time or another and it's not right to stare at the prisoners. They feel bad enough as it is."

Stranger than the strange surroundings were many of the men of the Legion themselves.

On the bunk opposite mine, the little paste-board card customary in the Legion described the owner as follows:

JEAN RASSEDIN
12429
SOLD AT PREMIÈRE CLASSE.

Rassedin was a Belgian. He worked as clerk in the regimental offices. Shortly before "soup-time" in the afternoon his day's work was finished. Then he would come running into quarters, tearing off his old white barrack uniform as fast as he possibly could, throwing his things pell-mell on the bed. In a very few moments he had put on the uniform prescribed for town. For the "soup" he didn't care. He never had his meals in quarters. He went away at once after he had changed his uniform and never returned before two o'clock in the morning, having a "certificate of permanent permission" to leave the barracks. His manner was haughty. If one of his comrades tried to speak to him about something or other, he usually turned away without answering. Or he said:

"*M'en fou*—I don't care for anything. Leave me alone."

Monsieur Rassedin, *légionnaire*, took his meals in the best hotel of the town and spent more money than any other man in Sidi-bel-Abbès. Rassedin was a rich man. From the standpoint of the Foreign Legion, his wealth was the wealth of Croesus. He had been a non-commissioned officer in a Belgian cavalry regiment, had deserted for reasons unknown and joined the Legion. After being a *légionnaire* for a time, he got the news of the death of a rich relative, who had left him all his wealth. . . . So Monsieur Rassedin, *légionnaire*, had become rich. He always carried a few thousands *francs* about him. Three men of the company were employed by him to keep his things in order and to do all the cleaning and polishing for him.

In the regimental office he paid the other clerks to do his work. He naturally preferred reading novels to copying lengthy reports. As he could afford to pay substitutes, the thing could easily be done. His family had succeeded in getting him a pardon granted for deserting. Monsieur Rassedin could have gone back to Belgium long ago, but he did not care to return to his native country. As soon as he had finished his term of five years' Legion service, he signed on again for another five years.

The reason?

"Disease," Smith said, when I asked him. There certainly was no question concerning men or things of the Legion that the man from California could not answer. "The poor devil's suffering from syphilis. Got it in Madagascar. I asked him once why in thunder he did not get out of this confounded Legion.

"'Bugler,'" he said in answer. 'You are an old *légionnaire* and I don't want to have trouble with you. But remember: You go your own way, and I'll go mine. Don't trouble me with your fool's remarks. There is poison in my body and in a few years I shall be very sick. No, I prefer putting a bullet through my brains in the Legion to returning to my country and then having to peg out. You'll die somewhere in the sand, my friend—I shall die strictly in my own fashion. What is the difference? Now come on, bugler. Want a bottle of champagne?'"

Everybody in Sidi-bel-Abbès knew Rassedin, even the little black children in the streets. Many a time he used to throw *franc* pieces amongst them.

In quarters Rassedin hardly spoke to anybody. His comrades were afraid of him. He was a man of enormous strength and had the reputation of fighting on the least provocation. But he could be very good-natured. Hardly a day passed without some old soldiers of the company coming to our quarters in search of Rassedin. They would simply rub their throats in pantomime:

"Rassedin, *tant d' soif.*—Heap big thirst."

Then Rassedin grinned and searched his pockets for copper pieces.

Then there was Latour, a Frenchman, serving his second year. Daily he received letters, a very unusual thing in the Foreign Legion; love-letters from a woman who was waiting for him five long years. Latour, who had committed a crime in France, expiated his deed in the Foreign Legion. He served solely for the purpose of "rehabilitation."

Sentences of the Civil Court are in France entered in the personal papers of the criminal. Without his papers he cannot get work. Naturally employers are shy of taking men who have been in conflict with the law and such a man very seldom succeeds in finding work. It is a barbarous system. Ten years must elapse before such a man is considered rehabilitated and "clean papers" are issued to him. If a man is willing to serve in the Foreign Legion, however, the term of rehabilitation is shortened to five years, and after five years' service new papers are given to him. He has then a new start in civil life after five years instead of ten.

Like many other French *légionnaires*, Latour was serving for rehabilitation.

The strangest man of all, however, seemed to me this man Smith, American, *légionnaire*, philosopher. I have always believed, and believe yet, that he actually loved the Legion, that he could not part from the strange life there. He could speak Arabic like a native. Many a time when we were lying in our bunks, he would mumble to himself in Arabic for hours. If I, in curiosity, asked him what he was about, he would say:

"Oh nothing, Dutchy. I'm a bit off my base. I very often am, you know."

But occasionally he would straighten up and sit down beside me, talking of strange things, reciting whole chapters of the *Koran*. Like this:

"Well, sonny, know anything about the Chapter of the Prophet's Stallions?"

"You don't? Listen."

"When of an evening the stallions, standing on three feet and placing the tip of their fourth foot upon the ground, were brought before the Prophet, he said: 'I have loved the love of things of this earth more than I have loved all thoughts of the things of heaven, and I have wasted the time in feasting my eyes on these horses. Bring them to me.' And when the horses were brought to him, he began cutting off their legs, one by one, saying: '*All' il Allah.*'"

"Yes, Dutchy, the *Koran's* something interesting."

Many chapters of the *Koran* I have learned from Smith.

Such things happened every day. But soon the enormities lost their power of fascination. A host of new impressions were forced upon me, until the senses were dulled and one soon got wonderfully indifferent—absolutely indifferent. . . .

CHAPTER 5

The Military Value of the Foreign Regiments

When in the twilight of awakening day the first red-hot rays of African dawn penetrated through the windows of our quarters, the *garde-chambre*, the man on duty there, arose noiselessly. He took good care not to make a noise, not from any delicacy of feeling on his part, but from the knowledge of the dire punishment which awaited him if he inconsiderately disturbed the sleep of his comrades. For the hours of sleep are a "Holy of Holies" to the *légionnaire*. When Herr von Rader was on duty for the first time, and in getting up made a slight noise, boots (heavy military boots!) were thrown at his head from all parts of the room, as a somewhat urgent reminder to be quiet.

In a few minutes the orderly returned from the kitchen dragging with him a large earthenware jug, lighted the petroleum lamp which hung in the middle of the room, and his voice then sounded loudly through the room:

"*Au jus.*" (Sauce.)

The sauce was coffee, strong, black, excellent coffee. Mechanically each *légionnaire* sat up in bed, and leaning on his arm mechanically felt behind him for the "quart," the tin mug, which hung on a hook at the head of the bed, handing it to the orderly, who went from bed to bed with his large jug and poured out coffee. The strong mixture soon dispelled all sleepiness, and when the shrill trumpet-blasts of the *réveillé* sounded from the barrack-yard, they all jumped out of bed.

Now began a *tohuwabohu* (pandemonium) of noise and hurrying to and fro. In half an hour the recruits had to muster in the yard. Corporal Wassermann, who liked to remain in bed until the last moment, called out continually:

"*Le—e—vez-vous donc.*—Get up."

Then he thundered out the famous "*Allez, schieb' los!*" of the Legion. The curious term has been introduced by German *légionnaires* and has passed into the vocabulary of Algerian French. Not only the soldiers continually used this funny mixture of German and French, but Arabs and negro children in the street, when they wanted to hurry each other up, shrieked out: "*Allez, schieb' los!*"

"*Allez, schieb' los! Pas du temps.* No more time!" roared the corporal. The day began with hurry and scurry. The primitive lavatory was on the ground floor of the barracks and one was obliged to run up and down four flights of stairs in order to wash oneself. There was not a minute to spare. The boots had to be brushed; the blankets and mattresses of the bed had to be folded neatly and piled up at the foot of the bunk. Whilst this was being done the orderly shouted excitedly:

"*Quoi! Nom de Dieu*—*balayez au-dessous vos lits!*" (Thunder and lightning! Sweep up under your beds.)

The etiquette of the Legion in these things holds very strictly to old tradition; every *légionnaire* had to sweep under his bed, while the cleaning of the room was the work of the orderly on duty, who could of course not begin this work until the floor beneath the beds had been swept. That was the reason of all the "*Quois*" and "*Nom de Dieus!*" The man had every cause to be excited and angry. He had to drill like the others, and it was no trifle to have to sweep a large room, to dust and to fetch water; everything within ten minutes. And it had all to be in tip-top order, for a few minutes before commencing drill the colour-sergeant inspected quarters and if anything was not in order in the room the corporal was punished.

And when the corporal was punished, he of course took care that his men were run in as well.

Punctually at 6 a.m. we recruits mustered in the barrack-yard in drill uniform: white linen suit, blue sash, knapsack, cartridge-belt and rifle—uniforms and leather trappings of shining brightness. The almost pedantic cleanliness of the Legion, the *coquetry* of each individual *légionnaire* to put a certain amount of *chic* into his uniform, was the first thing Corporal Wassermann's vanity had taught us.

In the quick easy marching pace of the Legion we went out to the *Plateau*, a large open space near the negro quarter, surrounded by olive-trees and red African oaks. The yellow clayey ground was stamped hard by the marching of many thousands of *légionnaires*. On the one side of the *Plateau* was the *village nègre*, the negro town. Close to the drill-ground the mosque, in proud white splendour, towered above the miserable, half-ruined huts of the negro quarter, and hour by hour sounded loudly from its minaret the priest's call to prayer:

"*All' il Allah.* God is great. . . ."

"*Arré, arré*—go on, go on," yelled the Arabs, who drove their heavily laden donkeys across the place with much scolding and beating. By the side of the donkeys, like the beasts, heavily burdened, walked Arab women, the legs bare to above the knee, but the face modestly covered as prescribed by the teachings of the Prophet. Only a small portion of the forehead was left free by the veil, and this was painted with a bright red round spot of henna, the sign of the married woman.

The Arabs glanced at us with timid side looks and hastened to pass on. Half-naked Arab and negro children raced about trying with comical *grandezza* to imitate the martial steps, and shouted Arab words at us which very likely were gross insults, until Corporal Wassermann picked up stones and drove them away.

"*Formez les faisceaux. Sac à terre.*" (Pile arms. Lay down your knapsacks.)

"*Pas gymnastique!*" (At the double!) "*En avant. Marche!*"

With this the daily routine began. It was the famous "Legion's breakfast," the lung-training of "double time."

In the form of a wide square we went round the drill-ground, five minutes, ten minutes—*un, deux, un, deux*—always in sharp time. The corporal, a splendid runner, ran at the head, teaching us the trick on which everything depended here, to overcome the critical moment of lung exhaustion, to get the "second wind." Even if the breath came and went in short pumping gasps, if the eyes pained, and one commenced to stumble from exhaustion, one ran on until the lungs had got used to the extra exertion, until one had the feeling of being a machine, and could go on running for ever. Then came the command "*A volonté*" (as you please)—and a race finished thirty minutes' exercise.

This is the Legion's breakfast.

It has cost many a man his lungs.

Pause. The tormented lungs worked in short hard gasps. It was impossible to stand still. One was obliged to walk up and down quickly in order to gradually quieten the pumping lungs.

The body had to expend all the strength it could in this morning drill. Swedish gymnastics, *le boxe*, formed the alternative to this doubling. The training progressed very quickly. All the recruits had served in some of the world's armies, and the first rudiments of military wisdom had been drilled into them long ago. Three-quarters of my fellow-recruits were Germans, who did not understand any French, and to whom the French commands were Greek. Continual repetition was here necessary.

"*A gauche—gauche* means left about" explained the corporal, and repeated it ten times, until *gauche* had been mastered. The most necessary French expressions were very quickly learnt by this most natural of all methods.

A hot sun burned down on us. Ten times during a single forenoon every stitch of clothes on one's body was soaked with perspiration, and ten times it dried again. In the pauses one stood about, smoking hand-twisted cigarettes, the inevitable cigarette of the Legion smoked in every free moment, and by which the pause is measured according to the old custom of the Legion? The pause was the duration of a cigarette. When the corporal had finished smoking his cigarette he slowly walked to a distance of about one or two hundred metres and lifted his hand:

"*A moi.*"

That meant we were to run up to him and recommence work.

"I've never run so d—— d fast in all my life," was Herr von Rader's continual lament. "I've an idea the suckers here are mistaking me for an express train!"

At 11 a.m. we marched back to barracks. Knapsack and cartridge-belt were thrown into the *paquetage*, and dead tired we threw ourselves upon our beds. But after a few short minutes, the soup signal rang out from the barrack-yard.

"*A la soupe, légionnaires, a la soupe, soupe, soupe.*"

"*Soupe . . .*" everyone yelled. Woe if the orderly of the room did not rush to the kitchen, and woe if he did not reappear with the soup-kettle in the twinkling of an eye! In everything connected with food a genuine *légionnaire* stands no nonsense—he has too often suffered starvation on marches and campaigns not to appreciate *la gamelle*.

The morning soup, the first of the two daily meals, was the same every day: Bread soup, boiled together, with potatoes and vegetables, and a piece of meat. With it the grey-white French military bread was served, and every other day a quarter of a litre of heavy red wine. The food was eaten off tin plates at the two long tables in our quarters. There was, however, not room enough for all at the tables. The question of seats the Legion's etiquette decided; the privilege of sitting down at table belonged to the old *légionnaires*.

After the soup the kitchen corporal rushed from room to room: "*Aux patates—aux pommes de terre!*" (To the potatoes !)

The whole company marched down to the kitchen, and standing in a large circle peeled the day's supply of potatoes. Everyone had to peel—he who had no pocket-knife had to make shift with a sharpened spoon-handle! The purchase of a pocket-knife was an exorbitant luxury on a wage of five *centimes* a day. . . .

In the afternoon the old *légionnaires* went off on long marches or to field practice, or were ordered to *corvée*, to work with spade and pick, whilst the recruits had instruction. At 5 o'clock in the afternoon, after a second *soupe*, which was exactly like the first, the official free time of the *légionnaire* began.

But in reality the most tiresome work of all now began—cleaning and washing!

Rifle cleaning, cleaning of uniforms, polishing the leather parts of the uniform. Leather! Even now I still think with a gentle shudder of the leather of the Legion, of the cartridge-belt and pouch! There is such a lot of trouble and work connected with these leather belts! The vainest *neuvaine* does not spend so much time over the whole of her *toilette* as does the *légionnaire* over the polishing of his cartridge-belt! The procedure was unutterably ridiculous, in the highest degree pedantic and unpractical, being irksome beyond all measure. You melted black wax over a match and put it on the leather. Then this wax had to be properly rubbed in with a flat piece of wood, till it was evenly distributed. Then began the real polishing with an arsenal of different rags. It took two hours to make cartridge-belt and pouch shine properly, till the *légionnaire*'s vanity was satisfied. . . .

Unpractical and old-fashioned as the *astiquage* is, it belongs to the etiquette of the Legion and is sacred. I had a special hatred of it and considered myself infinitely smart when I bought a bottle of leather dressing and simply painted my belts with it instead of working at them for two hours. It looked very well and was at all events more durable.

But Corporal Wassermann almost fainted when he saw it. He tore the belt out of my hand, and in a fit of rage ran round to all the men's rooms, to show the other corporals what horrible things happen in this sinful world. A painted cartridge-belt! The old soldiers of the companies came running up and with many "*merdes*" and "*noms d'un chien*" surveyed in petrified astonishment the greenhorn who had been so audacious as to attempt to supplant the sacred *astiquage* of the

Legion by painting!

"But it is more practical," I said at length to the fuming corporal in the vain attempt to appease him.

"*Mais, ça ne marche pas!*" he shrieked. "That will never do. If you were an old soldier and not a recruit, you would be locked up for ten days!"

The greatest plague, however, was the washing. The white uniform had of course to be washed every day. In the back barrack-yard was the *lavabo*, a large reservoir built of concrete, with cold running water, called in *légionnaire's* wit *cercle d'enfer* (Hell's circle). Every free hour the *légionnaires* stood shoulder to shoulder around the reservoir, in a large circle, shirt-sleeves turned up, with flushed and perspiring heads. Behind those washing other *légionnaires* waited patiently until a place at the reservoir became vacant. There they washed, rubbed, beat and rinsed until darkness set in. The white linen uniforms, the underclothing, and the linings of the uniforms had to be washed in cold water and with little soap. The small piece of soap which each man received once a month was not nearly enough, and few things were railed at as much as the lack of soap. Scarcely had one turned round, when lo and behold! the soap was gone.

Nothing represented the poverty of the Legion so much as this *lavabo*. The man who possessed a brush, an ordinary "washing-brush," and with this could simplify the work of washing, was as much envied as if he had been a millionaire—to lend such a brush was looked upon as an act of the greatest friendship! For drying purposes lines were hung up nearby, and when one had hung up the wet clothes, one waited patiently until they were dry. A man who was careless or impatient, and who did not do so but went away, might afterwards survey the place on the line where his washing had been hanging—the wash itself was gone, had disappeared, been spirited away.

With the half-dry wash one returned to the room, laid one's blanket on the table and "ironed" trousers and tunics by smoothing them with the sharp edge of the drinking-mug until they were free of creases. The poor devil of a *légionnaire* thus needed an hour for a piece of work which could have been done in a few minutes with the help of a flat-iron. But the foreign *légionnaire* is far too poor to possess such a treasure as a flat-iron.

The object of our training was twofold: the training for prodigious marching performances, and the education of the individual to complete military independence. The working programme of the

Foreign Legion, the whole of its military value, is embodied in these two ideas:

Brilliant marchers—independent soldiers.

In addition to these two advantages we have the financial consideration, on which the Foreign Legion's existence depends—the advantage of cheap, splendidly trained mercenaries, with whom the most daring military operations can be undertaken without consideration of the sacrifice of life involved. No nation, no parliament asks for an account of the dead. The Legion marches and acts independently, dies without attracting attention.

The *légionnaire* can march. Forty *kilometres* a day is the fixed minimum performance. He must be able to do that, day by day, without interruption, without a day of rest, for weeks on end. That is the object of his training from the very beginning—the daily *pas gymnastique*, the "double timing" in the long springy running stride of the Legion, the initiatory practice for marching. Several times every week the men must make practice marches over a distance of at least twenty-four *kilometres*, with full equipment, at the Legion's pace of five *kilometres* per hour, which has always remained the same.

The only object of the practice marches is to teach the recruits steady quick marching. They neither end with a small manoeuvre, nor have they exercises such as scouting, or exploring the country by means of patrols. It is nothing but simple marching at a prescribed pace, a tramping onwards to fulfil a given task. The *marches militaires*, as the practice marches are called, usually commence at midday, when the sun is at its hottest, after a hard morning's drill, so as to represent a practical exercise. On one of the military roads which branch off from Sidi-bel-Abbès in all directions, the march goes on until the twelfth *kilometre* is reached, and then the men are marched back again.

On the march a *légionnaire* may carry his rifle as he pleases, either shouldered or by the strap, just as is most comfortable to him; he may take off his knapsack if it hurts him, and carry it in his hand; he is not ordered when to open his coat or when to shut it. The officers do not worry the marching *légionnaires* with paltry orders, and they are allowed to sing or to smoke as they please. When there is a large puddle on the road, or when one side of the road is stony, the column turns off of its own accord and marches where the road is best. In the course of many a whole-day march I have not heard a single word from the officers, no orders except the short whistle signals, which mean: "Column, halt!" and "Column, forward march!"

As soon as the signal sounds for a halt, the front rows form front without orders, and every man sits or lies down during the halt as suits him best. The marches are regulated by the one principle: March as you like, with crooked back or toes turned in, if you think that nice or better, but—march!

It is always being drummed into the *légionnaire* that he is intended for nothing else in this world except for marching. If the pangs of hunger are gnawing at his stomach or thirst parches his tongue, that is so much the worse for him, but is no sort of a reason for his not marching on! He may be tired, dead tired, completely exhausted—but he must not stop marching. If his feet are bleeding and the soles burn like fire, that is very sad but the marching pace must not be slackened. The sun may burn till his senses are all awhirl, he must go on. His task in life is to march. The greatest crime that he can commit is to fail on the march. There is no such thing as an impossible marching perform-ance for the regiment of foreigners. Each individual is inoculated with the one idea, it is hammered into him, that he has to march as long as he can control his legs. And when he can no longer control them, then he must at least try to crawl.

It is a merciless system, which, however, produces wonderful sol-diers.

Inseparable from the march of the Legion is the baggage of the *légionnaire*.

The French foreign soldier marches with an equipment called the *tenue de campagne d'Afrique*. He wears splendidly made laced boots, white duck trousers held together at the ankles by means of leather gaiters, and the *capote*, the heavy blue military cloak. The cloak is put on over the shirt, without any coat underneath, and its tails are but-toned back behind, so that thighs and knees are left free, and an un-trammelled gait rendered possible, just as with the French soldiers. The only difference is that the *légionnaire* wears the *ceinture* round the body, the blue sash, about four metres long, of fine woollen cloth, which not only gives the body a firm support, but also does service as a tropical belt, indispensable in the sudden changes of temperature in Africa, where the glowing hot day is followed by an icy cold night. The red *kepi* has a white cover, and, as further protection against the sun, a thin linen cloth—the *couvre-nuque*, neck-cloth—is buttoned on to the *kepi*, covering the neck, ears and cheeks. There are consequently in the Legion comparatively few cases of sunstroke, which may sound rather surprising.

He carries a rifle and a bayonet, two hundred to four hundred cartridges, cartridge pouch and knapsack, and the *sac*. This knapsack is made of black varnished canvas with a unique system of straps, and has hardly any weight of its own. On the march it contains two complete uniforms, the *légionnaire's* linen and polishing cloths, partly in the inside and partly in *ballots*, in carefully prescribed bundles. Tent canvas and blanket encircle the knapsack in a long roll. The collapsible tent-sticks are stuck in at the side. On the top is fastened the *gamelle* and fuel for the bivouac fire. In addition each man also carries one ;of the saucepans of the company or pioneer's implements. Knapsack, rifle and equipment altogether weigh almost fifty kilogrammes; no soldier of any other army carries such a load.

With this kit he marches over sand under a burning sun, on very scanty rations. In barracks he gets a cup of black coffee on rising in the morning. At ten o'clock he gets his forenoon soup, at about 5 p.m. his afternoon soup. Two meals a day, both consisting of soup, in which are boiled all sorts of vegetables, a small piece of meat, and now and then a special vegetable as an extra, spinach, carrots or such-like. With this he eats the French military bread, a grey kind of bread which is very easily digested, undoubtedly nutritious, sufficient and palatable. When marching, however, the meat rations are dropped, and food consists almost exclusively of rice and macaroni. As a substitute for the bread he is served with a kind of hard ship's biscuit.

Marching always commences in the early hours after midnight. It then goes on uninterruptedly, with the hourly halts for rest of five minutes, until the task has been completed. This is a peculiarity of the Legion from which there is no deviation, even when in the field. Be the distance ever so great, it is covered in *one* march.

The *Légionnaire* marches. . . .

The Foreign Legion, as an old troop of mercenaries, works like a machine. The newly recruited human material is quickly adapted to the old, faultlessly working parts. In barrack life and on the drill-ground the officers stand in the background. For these stages they are superfluous, and their work is confined to paper reports or to an occasional visit to the drill-ground. While I was serving in the Foreign Legion I only came into close touch with the officers of my company on the march. We scarcely knew them; the captain came into the company's office in the forenoon, and was not seen again for the rest of the day. The education of the men and their whole training is left to the non-commissioned officers, above all to the corporals. They were themselves once trained in the same service and possess, with rare exceptions, great talent in training their men to be independent.

The system of the marches is brutal; the *légionnaire* must expend what there is in him of vital energy and human strength, but in the military service he is treated as a soldier, as a valuable soldier, whom one does not worry with pedantic demands and paltry red-tape affairs, but treats him in a sensible, I might say loving, manner, in order to draw from him the utmost he is capable of. From the military point of view he is really well treated.

During my training I did not once hear a word of bad language, and if a strong expression was used, it was done in fun. Every morning and every afternoon nine recruits of the eleventh were taken to a secluded spot, a shady avenue near the Plateau, and were taken in hand by a corporal and a *légionnaire, première classe*.

Every movement was explained to us, the purpose of every manoeuvre illustrated precisely, so that we knew why we had to make this or that exercise. The smallest details were all explained. It was not considered a crime if in lining-up one man was a trifle farther forward than the other; but if any man was awkward at boxing, that was considered a very serious thing, and he was drilled by himself until he grasped the fact that boxing was a most important matter, which sharpened wits and nerves. In the pauses the instructors spoke to us and explained a hundred little things. The gun had to be carried across the shoulder in a certain place, because that was the easiest way of carrying and balancing it. We were obliged to work hard, but never had the feeling of being bothered with anything unnecessary. It was practical work, the reason for which every one understood.

This was repeated on a larger scale when drilling in companies. Everything was directed towards the practical and useful; one was not drilled mechanically, but by practical methods. The company drill was hardly ever conducted by the officers, but by the colour-sergeant of the company.

Here the training of the individual to independence stepped in. In the course of the day every man was given a problem which he had to solve: the estimating of distances, the search for cover or ambush. . . . For instance, ten men were told off as a scout-patrol, and had to reach a certain spot without being seen. At the goal the whole company assembled, and every *légionnaire* could watch for himself how the scout-patrol carried out their task. Their movements were criticised by the watching *légionnaires*; in great excitement they debated if another way did not offer better cover, or if the patrol should not have remained longer at one point to get a wider range of view for their observations.

This military criticism was looked upon with favour, and sergeants and corporals regularly took part in the discussion. This introduced into the hard service a suggestion of sport and individual interest, stirring the ambition and giving interest to the work. For all that the general work of the troop was not neglected and drill was not despised when necessary. To my mind the firing discipline, for instance, was perfect.

"Being practical" was the leading principle of the whole training. Each man knew the length of his steps and knew that he required 117 or 120 or 125 steps to walk 100 metres. In interesting instructive lessons in the field the *légionnaire* learnt not only the rudiments of map-reading, but was taught to illustrate a report by a sketch, if it was only a rough one. The corporals took special pains with the talented and educated *légionnaires*, stirring their pride and ambition to achieve something out of the common. One had the feeling of working for a sporting competition.

On clear, starry nights the company was often alarmed and marched into the surrounding country of Sidi-bel-Abbès. Far out in the open field we stopped. These exercises were conducted by our first lieutenant. He gathered the *légionnaires* round him in a circle and explained to them the constellations, their movements and their relation to each other. This was repeated so often till even the greatest dunce could find his bearings by means of the Pole-star and the Great Bear.

Personal interest was brought into the soldier's work. One became independent, one knew the Why and the Wherefore. Again and again rifle-pits were dug, and sporting ambition urged us to work quicker than the next section.

There was equal competition at the frequent drills in throwing up earthworks, and with wonderful rapidity entrenchments were built up of haversacks filled with sand. It was like watching a match to see the *escouades*, the different sections of the company, endeavouring to be the first to have their tent up. With one pull they had the tent-cloth out of the knapsack, and fitted the sticks together; everyone had his own piece of work—the one buttoned the tent canvas together, the other stretched the sides down tight, and the next one drove in the pegs. And like a miracle the little tent grew out of the ground.

My squad held the record in tent-building with seventy seconds. It was looked upon as a matter of honour to turn out with the greatest speed and exactness, one was proud of being able to form square on the march in a few seconds. One ran like mad at the command "*A genoux!*" an interesting manoeuvre, the purpose of which was to save oneself from bursting shells and volley fire. When the command "*A genoux!*" (Down on the knees!) sounded the whole line in long strides moved closely together, every single man fell on his knees and put his head as far under the knapsack of the man in front of him as possible, each one crowding close to his neighbour. No head, no back was visible, nothing but a compact mass of knapsacks. The head of each man was protected by the knapsack of the man in front, this and his own knapsack protecting him from shells and shrapnel. The *sac*, with its contents of soft uniforms and underlinen, was proof even against a rifle-bullet.

Everything was practical. All the bother with the *paquetage*, the paltry and exact folding up of equipment according to a prescribed plan, meant in reality prompt readiness at shortest notice. The *légionnaire* has no wardrobe and is obliged to put a host of things into a ridiculously small space with methodical neatness. But the result of all this is that he can find every piece in the dark and stands with his kit packed according to marching regulations ten minutes after the alarm.

The Legion understands its soldiering business. One must admit that. It shoots brilliantly. The general regulations for the computation of the shooting range are absolutely ignored by the Legion. But every man tests his gun over every range until he knows exactly, when given a distance, how his own gun shoots over it: at four hundred yards, a hand's breadth up, and a hand's-breadth to the left . . . and so on. The shooting-range at Sidi-bel-Abbès is never unoccupied, cartridges are not stinted, and a company would feel very unhappy if at least half of its men were not first-class shots. Money prizes are even given. I once got a prize of ten *francs*. . . .

On the other hand, it is on the rifle-ground that one can see how the *légionnaire* is treated as a man. He is supposed to be a badly treated man, a desperate man, one not to be trusted. As a soldier the *légionnaire* must shoot, shoot much. As a desperate man he ought not to have arms in his possession. But the Legion has found a compromise. A corporal stands behind every *légionnaire* who shoots on the range, watching the shooter's every movement. From the same reason even the sentinels do not get any cartridges. The non-commissioned officer in command of the guard receives a small box with ammunition, locked and sealed and only to be opened in case of necessity. Is a sentinel attacked, then he must defend himself with his bayonet until he can alarm the guard and bring the officer on duty to the rescue with cartridges. Such things are significant. But they do not prevent the *légionnaire* from being a splendid soldier.

Individual training—Boer tactics—practical instruction . . . that is the Legion. And it marches. Now and then its marching powers are increased artificially. The *compagnies montées,* one with each regiment, companies mounted on mules, have even done seventy kilometres a day. Every two men have a mule. The one rides and takes the baggage of his comrade marching alongside with him on the mule. Then they change about. The mounted companies lie far in the south and follow up the hostile Arabs with colossal forced marches.

But on the whole *la Légion* depends on its legs. These brilliant professional soldiers march.

I will give you, naturally translated, my company's weekly programme as it was hung up on the blackboard every Saturday:

Monday .   6-7 Boxing.
            7.30-10 Company drill.
            12 Military march.
Tuesday .   6-7 Gymnastics.
            7.30-10 Skirmishing.
            11-12 Instruction in hygienic rules in the field.
            1 Work under the quartermaster's direction.
Wednesday. 5.30-6.30 Boxing.
            7 Company musters for bathing.
            8-11 Mending uniforms, preparation for inspec
                tion by the colonel.
Thursday.   5. 30 March to the shooting-range.
            12-1 Instruction in first-aid to wounded.
            1.15 Work under the quartermaster's orders.
Friday.   5 Military march.
            1-2 Instruction in taking cover in flat ground.
            2.30 Work under the quartermaster's orders.
Saturday.   5.30 Run over six *kilometres.*
            8-11 Company drill.
            12 Cleaning of barracks and quarters.
            4 Inspection of the barracks by the colonel. The
                men stand beside their beds in duck suit.
N.B.—At the 11 o'clock muster each morning a part of the

uniform, to be named each day by the adjutant, has to be presented for inspection.

Inseparable from the Legion's military value is the Legion's work.

Not so very long ago Sidi-bel-Abbès was a sand-heap, on which only a *marabout* stood, the tomb of a pious saint, to which the Arab hordes of the Beni Amer made pilgrimages. At that time strange men came, gathered round the brand new flag of the Legion and convinced the sons of Amer in bloody battles that it would be good for their health to move farther south. These strange men built roads and burned bricks. They built solid fortification walls, drained that horrid little rivulet Mekerra, which flowed so sluggishly through the sand, and which smelt so badly; they laid out gardens and planted olive-trees. The barracks, the public buildings, most of the dwelling-houses arose under the hands of these industrious mercenaries.

The *légionnaire* was always and is always still a workman. The heaviest work of the Foreign Legion is done on the smallest military stations in Algeria, down in the south, on the borders of the Sahara, where every day's bodily work means loss of health to a European. There the working column turns out day by day with pick and spade to build roads, whilst perhaps in an Arab village a few hours distant the civil authorities are distributing "relief" in the form of natural products to loafing Arabs. Eighty *per cent*, of Algeria's brilliant roads have been built by the Legion.

The trowel is thrust into the *légionnaire's* hand. There, now you are a mason. He builds barracks for the troops and offices for the civil administration. He breaks the stones with which the roads are repaired. He performs the pioneer work of Northern Africa at a wage which a *coolie* would scoff at.

His strength is made full use of. A grotesque example of this is the custom prevailing in the 2nd Regiment, stationed in Saida, to allow *légionnaires* to work for private people in the town. They, of course, get less wage for this than a common workman would ask for, but that in itself would not be so bad, because even the few *francs* a day mean wealth to a *légionnaire*. The peculiarity, however, the typical side of the whole affair, is that these workers have to hand over a part of their day's earnings to the funds of their company. The company enriches itself through their work.

In the garrison life of Sidi-bel-Abbès the work of the Legion took grotesque forms. In my life I have spent several weeks on end in the saddle; while still very young I struggled for existence in the United

States; I have suffered from hunger and cold, and for months I have had shivering fits of malaria—but I never experienced to such a degree the feeling that my physical strength was being pumped out of me to the last drop as during the time I spent in Sidi-bel-Abbès. I was always tired and every free moment found me stretched out at full length on my camp bed. During work I had the ambition (which today appears to me ridiculous) to be second to none in strength and endurance. Scarcely, however, was the work ended, when the bodily and mental depression set in.

My captain was quite right when one day at inspection he stood still in front of me and said disapprovingly to the sergeant: "*Il a maigri beaucoup!*" (He has got very thin!)

"*Mais il fait son service,*" replied the sergeant. (He does his work.)

That was of course the principal thing.

The getting thin and feeling tired had their own good reasons. Like all *légionnaires* I was a working animal. Early in the morning the hard military service began. The afternoon brought the *corvée* work, and the evening the ridiculous small jobs of the barrack routine. The word *corvée*, which literally means drudgery and in the military sense "work," I will not forget as long as I live, and will never read it again without shuddering. *Corvée* was a component part of almost every day in the Legion. The work was often so hard that every bone and every muscle in my body ached, often it was simply ridiculous and depressing.

The greater part of the company mustered generally at 1 p.m. in the barrack-yard, and the sergeant *du jour* chose working parties, each of which was in charge of a corporal. That was something quite different to the military service. Indifferent as I must have been at that time, I nevertheless always noticed the sulky and disgusted faces the men made when they went to this work. In small groups we marched out of the barracks, armed with broom, pick and shovel.

The Legion was there to work, and from the *légionnaire* one could ask things impossible in other French troops. If one saw a soldier working in Sidi-bel-Abbès, then he was sure to be a *légionnaire*. Arab *Spahis* or French soldiers of the line, who were also stationed in Sidi-bel-Abbès, had never such work to do as we did, and which should have been done by scavengers and navvies. That was the privilege of the Foreign Legion.

From the Arab *Spahis*, that is to say from the natives, such work was not demanded. On the other hand, the Legion had often to supply men to put the forage of the *Spahis* under cover. That may sound paltry, but it is just these small things that characterise the way the *légionnaire* is taken advantage of. He is just good enough for any kind of work.

We swept the public park of the town for the citizens of Sidi-bel-Abbès, whilst the gardeners stood idly by, watching us and ordering us about; we rooted out the undergrowth, and cleansed the brook which ran through the botanical gardens from mud and refuse. We emptied the drains in the officers' houses; we did scavengers' work in the filthy slums of the town.

Once I was a member of a detachment that had to clean the sewers in the Arab prison. The work was loathsome beyond measure. We had taken with us a large barrow with casks, and had to haul from underneath the floors of the cells and prison rooms the large tin pans, and carry them to the barrow. We performed this disgusting work, whilst in the prison yard the loafing Arab rabble prowled around and made jokes at our expense.

Sunday only was free from work, free from all kinds of service. We were not even mustered. And the *légionnaire* lies the whole blessed Sunday in bed. Towards evening he goes to the Jardin Public to listen to the concert given by the regimental band. He goes there because it is the Legion's custom—but he would much rather sleep on. . . .

CHAPTER 6

"The Legion Gets No Pay"

The poor fellows who enlisted because they had no money to buy a crust of bread made the biggest mistake of their lives when they thought to finish with their troubles by entering the Legion.

Without exception every man in the Legion had his money troubles.

Money was a thing of immense value in the Foreign Legion. The possession of a few *francs* made an enormous difference and created in the midst of the Legion's red-trousered equality the finest social grades and distinctions. Not only the value but also the power of money was enhanced in the Legion. Copper pieces meant a great deal here. Copper pieces purchased a few *litres* of wine, or a nocturnal *carouse*, or a substitute to help in doing hard work. The *légionnaire* with a little money was on quite a different footing to the man who had none.

Rassedin, the wealthy Rassedin, was a prince in a surrounding of poor devils. A wide gap parted him from the other men. They flattered him to get into his good graces and accepted gladly his insolence, if there were but a few *sous* or a few good cigarettes to be had. Of our quarters he was the king. He reigned supreme. He was obeyed in all matters. It was too funny to see how his comrades hurried themselves when this man, the incarnation of the God of Mammon in the Legion, happened to express a wish, and how they then went off with beaming faces to the canteen to change the couple of *sous* they had earned into wine.

The self-confidence with which the Belgian bore the dignity of his wealth (and what enormous wealth are a few thousand *francs* to a *légionnaire!*) was, considered by itself, only funny. But many a time I suspected that Rassedin, who knew so well what a frightful death was waiting for him, despised the petty greed of them all from the bottom of his heart.

Money rules even in the Foreign Legion!

The pay is five *centimes* daily, which is about one cent or one half-penny. Exactly the fiftieth part of the daily pay of an American regular. The twenty-fourth part of a British soldier's daily pay. The comparison is grotesque.

When one considers, however, that the man who enlists in the Foreign Legion sells his skin and is a *paid* mercenary, the comparison becomes astounding. The average *légionnaire* finds out in a remarkably short time that he has been a fool to enlist, that he is the victim of a system very near akin to slavery, that he is a working man without wages, a labourer without pay. An old French proverb says: *Business is getting the other man's money!*

And very substantial values is *La France* getting out of the *légionnaire*. With this poorly paid Legion, the French Republic protects the boundaries of her territory in Algeria and conquers the southern deserts step by step—in the everlasting wars in French Tonquin the Legion's troops are always ready for service. Fighting is not the only work of the Foreign Legion, however. Only one-half of the *légionnaire* is a real soldier. The other half of him is workman, carpenter, builder, road-maker. He works hard and he is so cheap a workman that no Chinese *coolie* can compete with him. He receives board and clothes—and a *cent* a day the cheap soldier of the Legion, this funny soldier of *fortune*. He can be made use of in the most terrible climates, for the most risky operations, simply because nobody troubles his head about him and because his officers have no account to render for his life or death.

The sum of money which his work with pick and shovel, with mason's trowel and carpenter's axe has saved the French Government in all these years must be enormous. And if a bullet, or sunstroke, or typhoid fever, or dysentery carries away a *légionnaire*, the only expense he is the cause of is the making of a hole in the sand. So cheap! Truly, France's Foreign Legion is a well-paying enterprise! Glorious soldiers and successful workmen are remarkably cheap at five *centimes* a day. . .

Every five days the *légionnaire* gets his wages paid. He holds five copper *sous* in his hand and must decide whether to buy cigarette tobacco, or cleaning materials, or a bottle of wine. It is only enough for one of these three. The purchase of a box of matches, which are monopolised in Algeria and cost five *centimes*, is a very grave financial problem. Therefore matches are scarce. Nowhere in the world is one so often asked for a match as in the streets of Sidi-bel-Abbès and in the Legion's barracks.

No wonder that the possession of a few silver pieces is something truly great for a *légionnaire*; no wonder that men like Rassedin rule as kings. Nowhere can the lesson of the value of money be so thoroughly learned as in the Foreign Legion.

The money troubles of the Legion are, of course, ridiculously petty troubles.

The luckiest man (considered from the Legion's point of view) is he who has kept up some sort of communication with home. The most appalling letters are then written to parents and relations and friends. Usually the poor devil of a letter-writer exaggerates a little, and his descriptions of famine and hardships are most moving. They must be very hard-hearted people indeed who do not acknowledge the receipt of such a letter with a small postal order.

Then there is joy in the land of Sidi-bel-Abbès. For a day, or a few days, or even a week, the prodigal son with the postal order lives like a king. He has his boots cleaned for him, and would not dream of making his own bed as long as his money lasts. A comrade does that for him, and in reward is graciously permitted to share a drink. *C'est la Légion!* To play the *grand seigneur*, if it is but for a day, is the average *légionnaire's* dream of happiness. He thinks it the finest thing in all the world to play at having a servant, if it's but for a day. . . . And this is the surest sign of the *légionnaire's* abject poverty. These lucky ones who receive a postal order occasionally represent the *crème de la crème*, the *élite* of society in the Foreign Legion. The others have to help themselves. They must "decorate themselves!"

This "decorating" is a fine art in the Foreign Legion. It is a mixture of work, cunning, brains, and theft.

"Decorate yourself!"

That is the sum total of an old *légionnaire's* wisdom, and these two words are the only advice that he gives, or indeed can give, to the newcomer. Make your life in the Legion as easy as possible is the meaning of this advice; take care that your tobacco-pouch stays full, that your uniform is in order and your kit complete, that you have as often as possible the three *sous* necessary for your litre of wine.

The way in which this "decorating" is carried out is a purely personal affair. . . .

My friend the bugler used to make gaudy *ceintures* from coloured

73

pieces of cloth and old leather-work, belts with crests and buttons of the Legion. He found good customers for his belts amongst the Arabs and occasionally amongst Spanish workmen in the little wine-shops of Sidi-bel-Abbès. In his special methods of decorating the old *légionnaire* developed an extraordinary business instinct. His transactions were not at all simple.

An Arab never parts with hard cash—after the time-honoured manner of his kind. So the bugler had to "trade." He would exchange his gaudy rags for a pair of pretty golden-bossed Arabian shoes, or a grotesquely carved Arabian stick, or a morocco purse of fine leather-work. Then Smith would constitute one of the *légionnaires* on orderly duty in the officers' mess his agent. Paying customers could easily be found amongst the young officers. The final result was always the same: many litres of the sweet heavy wine of Algeria into which all the copper coins of the Legion invariably change.

A *légionnaire* of the fourth company was generally known as "*l'homme des biscuits!*" His speciality was to gather in all the companies the biscuits given out twice weekly to complete the bread ration. They were like ship's biscuit and extremely hard. Most of the men would not touch them. So the biscuit man had a capital gathering ground, and in some cunning way, which he carefully kept secret, he took sack upon sack of these biscuits out of the barracks. In the market- place of Sidi-bel-Abbès he found plenty of customers. Others, less inventive, confined themselves to cleaning and washing for comrades better off than they. In some way every one tried to "decorate himself." . . . The main object in a *légionnaire*'s life is the getting together of a few coppers.

Decorating meant also occasional theft. . . . In matters of stealing the Legion draws the line very sharply. The theft of equipment, to replace lost or stolen parts, was considered absolutely respect- able and gentleman-like. There was no other remedy, as the man who loses something is punished severely.

Thieving "decorating" is a very simple thing and quickly learned.

"I've lost a pair of trousers!" cries the recruit in despair.

"That's nothing," says the old *légionnaire*.

"Curse it, what shall I do then?" wails the newcomer.

"Decorate yourself, you fool," says the old hand.

Whereupon the recruit (after receiving detailed instructions from the wise old soldier) walks into the backyard, where the washing is hanging out to dry, and waits in a dark corner with great patience for an auspicious moment. A lightning snatch and a pair of somebody's trousers hanging innocently on the line are his. He has decorated himself. It's immoral, of course. It's theft right enough. It's deplorable . . . but it is most convenient. The Legion does not worry about small matters of right or wrong. The Legion says: "Each for himself; why didn't you keep an eye on your washing, you fool!"

Now such a single theft of a single pair of trousers naturally is but the first link in a long chain of trouser-stealing. The man who has been robbed has no other remedy than doing likewise. And so on. . . . In a very few days hundreds of pairs of trousers change owners, until somewhere in the long chain someone is struck who buys himself a new pair. Somehow or other it all comes right!

The Legion considers this sort of theft sportsman-like and gentle-manly, a thing permitted, and it is a *point d'honneur* to be smart enough not to get caught by the rightful owner.

But woe to the *légionnaire* who should ever extend his decorating operations to tobacco or money or even bread. The whole company would form a self-constituted detective corps and find the culprit out very soon. The rest would be—silence and hospital!

During one of the very first nights an ugly scene took place which showed only too well how a thief is treated in the Legion. In the middle of the night furious shouting made me jump out of bed. Sleepily I looked about me. Around Rassedin's bed stood a group of cursing and gesticulating soldiers. I went up to them. Smith and three others were holding in grips of iron a fourth man who could hardly speak for terror. His face was white as chalk. Rassedin stood there in his shirt, staring hard at the man caught.

"You're from the tenth company?"

"Yes," stammered the man.

"What in hell are you doing in the eleventh then?"

"Been drinking—got into the wrong quarters—let me go—"

In the meantime all the men in the room had gathered and were standing around the group.

"*Nom de Dieu*—what a dirty fellow!" said Rassedin. "Listen, you chaps. I had my money in my trousers and my trousers were under my pillow. Just now I felt something moving near me, jumped up and caught hold. Do you know what I caught? This chap's hand. What do you think of that?"

"*Voleur!*" cried the bugler. "Thief!"

The word acted like a signal. All at once fists were clenched, a bayonet gleamed, a struggle arose, and a dozen men rolled on the ground. The scene lasted for perhaps a minute. Then all was still—the man from the tenth company lay there gasping and covered with blood. His face was black, so terribly was it bruised. A blow from the bayonet had split his cheek and a stream of blood flowed over his blue jacket. The guard came up and the fellow was carried into hospital.

"He wanted to steal my money! He wanted to decorate himself! "said Rassedin grimly. "For the present we've decorated him!"

The man lay in hospital for weeks. That was the end of it. That night's lynch-law in our quarters was not inquired into. The punishment of the thief rests in the hands of his comrades. So decrees the custom of the Legion. . . .

When it came to "decorating," Herr von Rader was in his element. The Legion's little ways had nothing mysterious for him. In a week the whole Legion knew him and respected him as a man of brains and resource. Every evening he went across to the canteen. Money he had not. But he juggled untiringly with empty wine-bottles, performed the most difficult conjuring tricks with *absinthe* glasses, and used to tell *Madame la Cantinière* (who understood a little German) the funniest stories. Very soon he succeeded in making a deep impression on that worthy lady, the queen over so many desirable wine-casks. She found the clever Herr von Rader amusing, and she did something that she had never done before in her life. She gave the man of many tricks a *gratis* bottle of wine every evening, and into the bargain the change out of an imaginary ten-*sous* piece. Madame's Portuguese husband had no idea of this little secret of his wife's kind heart. Anyway, he need not have troubled himself: Herr von Rader had not the slightest intention of endangering *Madame la Cantinière's* conjugal fidelity—he only loved her wine. . . .

Thus did Herr von Rader decorate himself with his glib tongue and his clever fingers. The soldiering part of his work was easy enough for him. Herr von Rader got on better under the flag of the Legion than all the other recruits. Sometimes, however (when *Madame la Cantinière* was in a bad temper or her Portuguese husband kept too sharp an eye on her), even Herr von Rader would fall into a thoughtful mood. Then he would rub away angrily at his leather equipment and propound practical philosophy. Something like this:

"*Nom de Dieu!*" (Herr von Rader was already quite at home with the curses of the French language.) "*Nom de bon Dieu!* This Legion is no good. *Nix* good. Now, for an intelligent man like me there is a bottle of wine and a cigarette easily to be had anywhere in the world. You'll admit that! Is it easy here? It is not! I've got to waste a lot of thinking and fine art just to keep in cigarettes. . . . This Legion's rotten. I've been had. They've swindled me! I'll tell you what, *mein Freund*: I'm going to skin out. This boy is going to run away. ..."

He did "skin out," some time afterwards. For it the cheerful Herr von Rader was to suffer the whole immeasurably hard punishment system of the Legion.

Even this cheerful fellow, who knew so well how to help himself, and in consequence was far better off than the other men in the Legion, was troubled by the simple problem of the Foreign Legion! A problem which so many of the Legion's soldiers have tried to reason out with so many head-shakings. A problem which once an Arabian *Spahi* put very plainly in a few scornful words:

"The Legion works—the Legion gets no pay!"

CHAPTER 7

The City of the Foreign Legion

En ville! Off to Sidi-bel-Abbès! Every afternoon shortly before six o'clock there began a very exodus from the Legion's barracks to the town. A *légionnaire* would rather clean and polish for an hour after lights out in the semi-darkness of the night-lamp than miss his stroll to town. The daily walk in Sidi-bel-Abbès was part of the Legion's sacred tradition. At five o'clock the gigantic gates of the barracks were closed and only a little side door remained open. Here the sergeant of the guard posted himself and carefully inspected everybody who wanted to go out, so that the Legion's reputation for *chic* should not suffer. The uniform to be worn in town was prescribed every day by a special regimental order; each *légionnaire* had to wear the same uniform, red trousers and bluejacket or white trousers and blue overcoat, and everybody took an especial pride in looking as trim and smart as possible.

Three thousand soldiers of the Legion used to stroll about the streets of Sidi-bel-Abbès every evening. For me this daily walk was a wondrous change from the Legion's routine. Above the gleam of the electric arc lamps shone the starry glory of a southern sky. Little black boys in white breeches, whose countless folds might have told endless stories of stolen trifles they had concealed, lounged at the street corners and cried the evening paper, the *Echo d'Oran*; Arabs in white *burnouses*, carrying in their hands the dangerous Arabian sticks, in which they find a never-failing missile, stood motionless, silently watching with looks of suspicion the *Rumis*, the white foreigners who will always remain foreigners to them and whose customs they will never be able to understand. All Sidi-bel-Abbès was promenading; citizens of the town, officers and civilians of the *Bureau Arabe* with their womenfolk. In between came the Legion's heavy soldier-steps and the sound of gently rattling bayonets.

Four streets, which run exactly north, south, east, and west, to Oran, Daya, Maskara, and Tlemcen, divide the town at right angles. They are the main streets in which the European shops and fashionable *cafés* lie. For private financial reasons the *légionnaire* does not buy in these shops and in the fashionable *cafés* he is badly treated. The *légionnaire* has no business in the main streets—from the honest citizen's point of view.

Between the blocks of the main streets, however, a labyrinth of small courts and alleys is hidden. There the Spanish Jews and Arabs live, there trading and bargaining goes on incessantly.

In this maze of dark alleys the men of the Legion were at home, in the treacherous wineshops which depended on the custom of the soldiers. "*Bar de la Legion*," or "*Bar du Légionnaire*," or "*Bar de Madagascar*" these hovels called themselves. Good wine is ridiculously cheap in Algeria. But out of the *légionnaires* extra money must needs be made. They were given a brew in the wineshops made from grapes which had been pressed already two or three times and to which a little alcohol lent flavour and "aroma."

Beside the wineshops were Mohammedan restaurants in which one could eat *kuskus* and *galettes*, tough pancakes with honey; restaurants in which knives and forks were looked upon as accursed instruments, which doubtless the devil of the *Rumis* must have invented for devilish purposes unintelligible to a true believer. Poverty and filth reigned in these places, but they were good enough for the poor despised *légionnaire*. One *café* in this quarter had an individuality of its own, depending exclusively on the custom of the Legion.

In a corner by the theatre a pretty little Spanish girl had put up a wooden hut and filled it with rickety old chairs, to be treated and used with great care, given her in charity probably somewhere or other merely to get rid of them. There she sold coffee to the soldiers of the Legion. This little woman had a good eye for business. Her coffee was, 'tis true, merely coloured hot water and not especially good water at that, but the soldier of the Legion willingly drank it, for Manuelita's coffee was very cheap indeed, and a pretty smile and a coquette glance went with each cup. When business was slack the hostess would even chat a little.

These tactics secured for the sly little Spaniard the faithful custom of the *légionnaires*. *La Legion* made love to Manuelita unceasingly. . . . The old *légionnaires* stole flowers for her, and if somewhere in Tonquin or on the Morocco border plundering had been going on, Manuelita would some months later be sure to receive the finest presents, stolen for her by her old friends of the Legion and carried about all the time in knapsacks. The Legion was grateful to Manuelita. She was the great exception. Besides her and *Madame la Cantinière* there was no woman in the town of the Foreign Legion who would even in her wildest dreams have deigned a *légionnaire* worthy of a glance.

Smith would never have patronised this *Café de la Legion*. He knew something much better. To him I owed my acquaintance with Ben Mansur's coffee. His was a Moorish coffee-house. Finely coloured mosaics formed Arabian proverbs on the floor and against the walls there were long marble benches. Arabs crouched on these benches and smoked comfortably gurgling *narghiles*—the incarnation of quietude and silence. For hours they sat over a single cup of coffee, whose purchase gave them also, according to Arabian custom, the right of spending the night on the marble benches. In stolid silence they played *esch schronsch*—chess.

One seldom saw a soldier of the Legion here, for Ben Mansur only spoke Arabic. Smith, however, was his bosom friend, and these two always greeted one another solemnly with deep bows, with their arms folded on the breast in Arab fashion.

Ben Mansur's coffee was a dream of fairyland. All day and all night charcoal glowed in the ancient Moorish stove in the corner, and in a wonderful octagonal copper kettle, which must have done service for generations of Arabs, there simmered boiling water. A silver can contained a thick coffee brew, a kind of extract. From this Ben Mansur filled the little clay cups half full and poured in boiling water. Then he conjured dreamland into the tiny little cups, adding a drop here and a drop there from mysterious bottles, a drop of essence of oranges, a drop of *hashish* oil and a drop of opium. Ben Mansur's coffee, with its wonderful aroma and the restful oblivion which that little cup gave, was a wonder never to be forgotten.

Smith and I used to sit on the marble benches by the hour, legs crossed in honour of the customs of our host's race. Before us stood the water-pipe of the Orient, a *narghile*, filled with wonderful tobacco very different from the products of the Algerian tobacco monopoly. Ben Mansur would never take more than two *sous*, which is two cents, for both of us, no matter how many pipes we smoked or how many cups of coffee we drank. This was his idea of hospitality.

Then again I used to wander with Smith through the dirty streets of the Jewish quarter, where the rubbish-heaps lay in the open streets and the atmosphere was tainted with every variety of smell. At the corners thin Spanish Jews, with the sharp features common to their race, haggled over a bargain; Algerian Jews walked stately through the alleys, in long flowing robes of blue and brown silk, men of importance who held the wealth of the country in their hands as the go-betweens of the world's trade and the riches of Algeria. Wealth and power dwelt in this miserable quarter of Sidi-bel-Abbès under the shell of poverty with which Israel is so fond of surrounding itself.

In the Ghetto of Sidi-bel-Abbès no trifle is so small that it is not worth haggling about, and no proposition paltry enough to come amiss to the man of the Ghetto, whose love of money is so great that he does not despise even the Legion's small copper pieces. The Ghetto and the Foreign Legion have quite lively business connections, consisting principally in the change of small currency notes. Many banknotes which originally formed the kernel of a *légionnaire*'s letter from home have wandered into the mysterious channels of Jewish trade. The Ghetto of Sidi-bel-Abbès has earned a small fortune in these small transactions.

A *légionnaire* is seldom much of a man of business and he certainly is always in a big hurry to get his dollar or his five *marks* or his five *pesetas* changed into *francs* and *centimes*—so he submits with more or less grace to fantastic rates of exchange, getting little more than three *francs* for a dollar and about four *francs* for a *fünf Mark Schein*. All other business of the Ghetto with the soldiers of the Legion is equally profitable—for the other man, be it understood, not, of course, for the *légionnaire*. Very often men of the Legion steal, under cover of darkness, silently through the little streets of the Jewish quarter carrying big bundles of brown woollen blankets and blue sashes, stamped in the middle and at the corners with the Legion's stamp in white paint, which marks them clearly as regimental property. But what's in a stamp! It can be got rid of easily enough with good will and a little turpentine. . . .

Anything that a *légionnaire* may want to sell the second-hand merchants of Sidi-bel-Abbès buy; at prices below contempt, it is true, but all the same they buy it. The small silver coins of the Ghetto have been the ruin of more than one soldier of the Legion who in a fit of rage sold his uniform to the obliging trader and paid the penalty with a long term of imprisonment.

Thus the interests of the Ghetto and the interests of the Legion are identical in a small way, and as a result the Ghetto man and the soldier are quite friendly with each other.

The honest citizen of Sidi-bel-Abbès, however, a half-caste of Spanish or Levantine or French extraction, is anything but fond of the red-trousered foreigner. He despises the Legion and its men from the bottom of his heart and has quite forgotten that the very same Legion built his town for him in the beginning; that there would be no Sidi-bel-Abbès if there had been no Legion.... His womankind draw their skirts close about them when they meet a *légionnaire* in the streets, as if he were plague-stricken. He himself why, he has managed to bring it about that the officers mess is now merely used as an evening club, while the officers have to dine in hotels, in order that the honest citizen may make a little money out of them.

The sub-lieutenants dine in one hotel, the first lieutenants in another, the unmarried captains and higher officers patronise a third. Every hotel had to have a share in the spoils, of course! The honest citizen is very indignant when the regimental band does not give a concert three times weekly for him; he has his public parks swept by the Legion and takes good care that all the provisions for the three thousand soldiers are bought in the town itself and nowhere else. For the trifling purchases which even a poor devil of a *légionnaire* sometimes makes he keeps a specially rubbishy class of article and charges double prices for it.

The regiment of foreigners is a very good thing for the honest citizen of Sidi-bel-Abbès, but nevertheless he despises the Legion and the *légionnaire*—this citizen of the Foreign Legion's town.

He takes good care, however, not to express his feelings of dislike too openly to Monsieur le *Légionnaire*, for he has more than once learnt that the men in red trousers are not to be trifled with. That they are much better left alone, in fact. The much-tried patience of the Legion has its strongly defined bounds and sometimes it gives way. When the Legion is not occupied in Tonquin or Madagascar or some such lovely neighbourhood, the regimental band gives a concert several times a week in the Place Sadi Carnot. The good man of Sidi-bel-Abbès always found this concert very fine, but what he did not like about it was that besides himself thousands of *légionnaires* promenaded in the Carnot square, enjoying the band's music as much as the civilians.

One day the honest citizen drew a cordon of police around the Place Sadi Carnot, with orders to let no soldiers pass, and thought he would now have the music all for himself....

The *légionnaires* were struck dumb with astonishment at this unheard-of impudence and the Arabian policemen felt very uncomfortable. News of the "outrage" was sent to barracks and in a very few minutes the men of the Legion were assembled in full force, discussing in fifteen different languages the evident impossibility of living in peace with the honest citizen of Sidi-bel-Abbès. All at once an old soldier gave the word of command:

"En avant par colonne du régiment—marche!"

The Arabian policemen tumbled to right and to left, the citizens of Sidi-bel-Abbès vanished as if by a conjuring trick into the side streets, and in five minutes there was not a single soul in civilian clothes to be seen on the Place Sadi Carnot. The men in red trousers held the field in triumph.

Since they were in fine humour and out for a real good time they promptly smashed up all the chairs on which the ladies and gentlemen of Sidi-bel-Abbès had been sitting, made a pile of them and lit up a grand bonfire while the regimental band played its gayest marches.

In the meantime a deputation of citizens had! rushed to the colonel of the regiment and made a great noise about these horrible *légionnaires*. The colonel merely laughed.

"My good sirs," said he, "it is now eleven o'clock. My men have leave till midnight. In another hour all will be over."

"But they have burnt the chairs," wailed the deputation.

"I'm very glad they have not burned anything else," laughed the colonel. "You leave my men in peace and they'll let you alone."

Since that time the honest citizen of Sidi-bel-Abbès has been rather more careful in his treatment of the Legion. It is true that an order of the town council says that a *légionnaire* can only get a ticket for the gallery in the town's theatre but if a *légionnaire* with superfluous money wants a seat in the stalls, he can nevertheless get it The honest citizen has learnt to respect the Legion's feelings.

But, under the surface, the citizen's contempt of the Legion naturally remained. The soldier of the foreign regiment puts out the fires which break out in Sidi-bel-Abbès, he saves the citizens and their goods when the stream of the Mekerra becomes a roaring torrent in the rainy season, and he protects the helpless townspeople when the descendants of the Beni Amer try to institute the Jewish persecutions they are so fond of. . . . He does all that. But the poor devil of a mercenary has no money, and this is the Mortal Sin.

One quarter of the town was taboo to us *légionnaires*, strictly forbidden under a penalty of a month's imprisonment: the village *nègre*, the negro town, the home of every sort of disease and crime. The beasts in human forms which house there had more than once killed a *légionnaire* to rob him of his sash or some such trifle.

Forbidden things always have a mysterious power of attraction, and I was burning with curiosity. Slowly, keeping a sharp look-out for patrols, I crossed the big drill-ground one night and turned, close behind the mosque, into the maze of huts. It was a pitch-dark night, and I kept falling over the dirt-heaps and tripping in the holes in the hard trodden ground.

At last I saw lights. The main street of the village *nègre* lay before me, a narrow little alley. I could have touched the walls on either side with outstretched arms. The miserable low houses were half in ruins, and irregular holes took the place of doors and windows. The alley, but a few paces long, was brightly illuminated by the light of half a dozen torches stuck in holes in the walls.

In this narrow space the vice of Sidi-bel-Abbès was hidden. Songs and cries and shrieks filled the air. Before the huts women were sitting, poor prostitutes, who sold themselves for a few coppers and a drink of *absinthe*. Here was vice in its most primitive form. The night was cold. Braziers with glowing coals stood before every hut, and women crouched over them that they might better warm their bodies at the warmth of the fire. Modesty seemed to be a thing unknown. A negress with a figure full of strength lay there stretched at full length almost naked, with the warmth-giving firepan beside her. She was too worn out or too lazy to speak, she merely invited the passers-by with a gesture to come into her hut.

Near her a Frenchwoman, in whose face her awful life had cut deep furrows, sat in a torn silk dress on the bare ground. Beside them Arabian girls crouched, children almost, the copper bangles on their arms and legs showing that they were from the far South. Italian women, with the characteristic gold earrings of their race, and Spaniards, with oily shining hair, quarrelled in high-pitched voices. The blazing light of the torches gave their faces an uncanny look. In the midst of these miserable women moved the scum of the population of Sidi-bel-Abbès. There were negroes in ragged linen coats who in daytime carried heavy burdens on their backs and spent their evenings regularly in the village *nègre*. Spanish labourers chattered and gesticulated with the Spanish girls. It was the meeting-place of the poor and the wretched, a *corso* of humanity at its worst.

My bayonet rattling gently against the steel sheath startled the men and women. When they saw that they only had to deal with a single *légionnaire* and not with one of the much-feared patrols, they cried out to me from all sides—in a curious *patois* of low French mixed with Arabic. The little I understood of it was quite enough. The language of the *légionnaire* leaves nothing wanting in the way of force and clearness—the language of the village *nègre* was filth condensed. Two negresses began to quarrel as to whether a common *légionnaire* could be in possession of even one *sou*, a weighty question which was answered in the negative amid much laughter. The Frenchwoman, who was anything but sober, poked me in the ribs and begged me, hiccoughing, for a *petite absinthe*. Obscene gestures and drunken cries everywhere. And in the corner there leaned in dignified repose an Arab policeman.

It smelled of *moschus* and heavy sweet Arabian cigarettes. In Arabic the alley was called the Street of the Seven Delights. Smith had told me that. One could but shudder at the contemplation of the seven delights. . . .

Then the comedy became clear to me. The honest citizen of Sidi-bel-Abbès despised the soldier of the Legion—but he tolerated the horrors of the village *nègre*.

Short commands sounded from afar and the steady steps of a patrol drew near. If I was discovered, it meant prison for me, so I dived into the protecting darkness of a small by-street. Stumbling and falling continually I felt my way forward in the pitchy darkness, till I heard low voices. The alley took a sudden turn.

I found myself in the court of a Moorish house. Arabs in white robes crouched and squatted on the ground smoking their *narghiles*. Most of them hardly looked up as I came in, and an old man with a long white beard nodded and smiled to me.

On the glowing fire stood a copper kettle with bubbling hot water, and an old negro was making tea for the Arabs. On the wall on one side of the court a cloth was hung up, of fine brocade, with golden embroidery, on a ground of red and yellow, in fantastical *arabesques*. Many cushions were spread on the white sand. The Arabs themselves sat on finely woven yellow mats. At respectful distance from the men girls stood and lounged about, wondrous youthful forms with veil-like robes and countless copper ornaments on arms and legs, which tinkled at their slightest movement. All were sipping tea out of tiny little cups. All at once I heard English words, an old nursery rhyme:

Humpty-Dumpty sat on a wall,

Humpty-Dumpty had a great fall,
And all the king's horses and all the king's men
Could not put Humpty-Dumpty together again.

Startled, I turned round and saw in the folds of an Arabian *burnous* the face of a white woman with fair hair and features who must once have been beautiful. Smoking an Arabian cigarette, she nodded dreamily with a happy smile and ever anew she would sing the nursery rhyme. . . .

Suddenly a girl sprang up, bracelets jingling, a child almost, of the pure Arabian type. Fascinated, the Arabs and the other women stared at her; so still it was that one could hear the sound of one's own breathing. The girl let the thin veil of a garment she was wearing fall down to her hips and stood immobile as a statue for a minute or two, her arms stretched out, the head proudly thrown back, her eyes shining in triumph courting admiration. She reminded me forcibly of a bronze statuette I had possessed in days gone by. . . .

Very slowly the child of the South began to dance. The delicate veil swayed and waved in ever-changing folds around her body of pure copper colour. Her dancing was wondrously graceful—it was beautiful beyond dispute. A strange scene it was, enhanced by the very bright colours and the heavy sweet smells of mysterious perfumes.

I stared in wonder at the dancing of this child of Nature and the wonderful rhythm of her movements. Faster grew the dance, the swinging and circling and posing. Suddenly the girl seized one of the torches and swung it in broad circles around her head. The firelight fell with its ruddy glow on her shining hair of black-blue. The hissing torch seemed to be enveloped in the swaying veil; ever faster grew that mad whirling. After a final lightning circle of the torch the girl fell down exhausted. . . .

A low murmur of applause arose from among the Arabs and many silver coins were thrown to her on the mat.

The woman who had sung the English nursery rhyme sat there as one stunned; she had forgotten herself and forgotten her surroundings. "My God," she kept on murmuring, "my God . . ."

I stole away and went slowly home to barracks, worn out.

A flowery belt of gardens surrounds the town. In broad alleys, which had been trenches in days gone by, stood groups of palm-trees and olive groves, planted by the soldiers of the Legion many years ago in the short intervals of peace. The botanical garden of Sidi-bel-Abbès had also been founded by the foreign mercenaries, and, to this day, (at time of first publication), the Legion has the right to gather flowers from the beds of the Jardin Public for its dead, and sends three soldiers daily to keep the paths in order and work for the gardener.

In return for this the regiment considers the Jardin Public its own private property, and on Sundays that wonderful garden, with its wealth of foliage and flowers, is the scene of a red-trousered invasion. Not very far from the Jardin Public lies the regimental garden, where the Legion raises its vegetables and plants its potatoes. I found it very funny when I was for the first time commandeered to carry dung in the Legion's garden—it seemed to me a most peaceful occupation for a modern mercenary. . . . Far out stretches the long line of flower gardens, with their narrow foot-paths shaded by olive-trees.

Right at the end of the town, where the gardens come to an end and the sand begins, there lies the cemetery of Sidi-bel-Abbès. Its showy monuments, its well-kept flower-beds, and its silent groups of trees do not give it any particular claim to individuality. If you pass through the churchyard, however, you will come to a large open space. Many hundreds of grave mounds lie there. The black wooden crosses are one like the other. This is the last resting-place of the Foreign Legion's dead. The Legion's churchyard. I was once commandeered to work there. An aged corporal, who lived in a cottage in a corner of the cemetery, and in the days of his old age filled the post of gravedigger to the Legion, gave me gardening tools and a watering-can. I walked along the long rows of graves, pulling out weeds and watering the grass. An indescribable feeling of loneliness overcame me.

So impersonal, so poor, so barren are those graves! They lie quite close together as if even in death the *légionnaires* must be drawn up in line for parade. The crosses are so small, so roughly painted, that one cannot get over the feeling that sordid economy is practised even on the last resting-place of the *légionnaire*. The crosses are hung with wreaths made of glass beads and with an artificial flower here and there. The name of the dead man is written on a small piece of board and underneath the name stands his number. To this comes the laconic addition: "*Legion étrangère.*" I felt sorry for these poor fellows who even in the last sleep of death had to bear a number which reminded one of a convict prison. I went from cross to cross and read the various names. Almost every nation in the world has contributed to the graves in the cemetery of the Foreign Legion, though the German names on the little crosses have a large majority.

A regiment of dead soldiers lies buried here. But it is only a small fraction of the Legion's dead. The others sleep somewhere in the sands of Africa—where they fell. Thirteen hundred *légionnaires* lie buried in Mexico. Hundreds and thousands rot in the swamps of Madagascar. Indo-China has been the death of hundreds of others.

The wind swept the dead leaves which fluttered across from the cemetery of respectability over the graves of the *légionnaires*. I looked at the endless line of grave mounds and at the meaningless numbers. And I thought of an old German song:

Verdorben—gestorben . . . Ruined—dead!

CHAPTER 8

A Hundred Thousand Heroes a Hundred Thousand Victims

Close by the prison, parted from the little square of sand and gravel, which formed the prisoners' exercise-ground, by a low brick wall, there stands the Legion's hall of honour.

A tiny little door is built into the wall and bears the inscription "*Salle d'honneur.*" Day and night there stands a sentry with fixed bayonet before the regiment's holy of holies. For the soldiers of the Legion it is forbidden ground, and the officers only gather there on festive occasions.

Late one evening I stole through the little gate. The sentry on duty was a man of my own company, whom I bribed with a packet of cigarettes to let me through.

I found myself in a tiny garden. Fantastic figures in mosaic work covered the ground; everywhere were dense groups of palms and laurels, and a broad flight of steps led up to the vestibule in Moorish style. As I entered the hall a flood of colour met my gaze. The walls of the enormous room were covered with pictures. Flanking the entrance were the life-size portraits of two *légionnaires*, the one in modern African campaigning kit, and the other in the uniform of 1815, of the "*Légion d'Hohenlohe.*" On the walls were the portraits of all the regiment's commanders and of the officers killed in battle. The names of the dead were inscribed on a marble slab in golden letters.

I noticed with astonishment that the Foreign Legion's list of commanding officers contained many names unmistakably German. There were the Colonels Stoffel, de Mollenbeck, Conrad, de Hülsen, and Meyer. And in very good company were these German soldiers of fortune: the list showed the names of some of France's most famous soldiers and generals. Each of them had at some time or other commanded the Foreign Legion, each had won his first military laurels leading the regiment of strangers: men famous indeed, the Legion's pride: MacMahon, Canrobert, Bazain, de Négrier, Saussier. . . .

Numerous pictures of battles represented episodes in the fights in which the Legion had taken part, and now and again among these paintings were real works of art. A number of these pictures come from the brush of Captain Cousin, while the allegorical *frescoes* on the ceiling are the work of an artist who wore the red breeches and blue coat of a common soldier. The *légionnaire* Hablutzel—the artist who decorated the *Salle d'honneur*—was a humble ranker.

In the French Army the Legion's varied talents are famous, and there are several stories besides that of this humble artist. The history of the Legion can tell of many such as he.

Five years ago the officers determined to build a new mess. There was only one objection to the fulfilment of this wish: the regimental coffers were well nigh empty. It was the colonel's idea to seek help in the regiment itself. In spite of the fact that the garrison at that time consisted of only one battalion, it was found on inquiry to contain no less than seven architects. These seven soldiers became once more seven artists, and executed the plans for the new officers' mess. They agreed on the style of a Tonquin *pagoda*. Among the Norwegians of the regiment were several carpenters who were experts in artistic woodwork; there were more than enough builders and masons to be found, and the bankrupt owner of a brickfield was glad enough to return for a time to his old profession and assume the direction of a section told off to make bricks. In a few weeks the mess was ready—its cost was solely that of the raw material.

The seven architects then once more shouldered their rifles.

There is another famous instance. In one of the countless fights in Southern Algeria, a company got cut off from the main column and suffered heavy losses in a scrap with the Arabs. The number of wounded was very great, and nothing could be done for them, as the doctors and bearers were with the main column. At last the captain in the thick of the firing called out to his men:

"Are there any doctors among you?"

Three *légionnaires* at once stepped forward. One was a graduate of the Sorbonne, another had gained the diploma of the University of Zurich, and the third had attained to the rank of M.D. at a German University.

Less strange, perhaps, but just as interesting, is the fact that for the building of a fort in the Legion three fortification experts reported themselves from a single company: two quondam Austrian pioneer officers, and a lieutenant from the British Royal Engineers.

General de Négrier, who loved the Legion, used to say that *les étrangers* had three inestimable advantages: they were brilliant fighters, they marched till they dropped,—and there was nothing that they could not do. He would undertake to build an engine with his *légionnaires*; from their ranks he could assemble the faculties of a university; there were men among them who could not only fight through a war, but they could also write its history.

The fact that the Foreign Legion's band is the best in the French army, and that it came back covered with glory every time it went to Paris to give concerts, is another proof of the many-sidedness of the Legion's talents. Many an artist who once played in the orchestra of one of the world's famous theatres afterwards carried the Legion's trumpets on his heavy-laden haversack.

I hardly need to emphasise the fact that these *légionnaires*, who, by virtue of their professions and social standing, belonged to a different class of society, always represented the exceptions, and that the majority of the men in the Legion were very simple fellows, whose past had nothing at all interesting about it. It is always the exceptions that one notices. An editor of the *Temps*, who visited Sidi-bel-Abbès and struck up a chance conversation with me, said in astonishment:

"I was speaking just now to a professor of Greek, and now you're a journalist. Is the Legion then a collection of ruined talents?"

In between the paintings in the *Salle d'honneur* there stand the Legion's memorial tablets, with the names of the battles in which the Legion took part written on them: forty-eight great battles, fought in all corners of the earth, from Indo-China in the East to Mexico in the Far West. The most disastrous fight in the annals of the regiment was that of Camaron, in Mexico, on April 30, 1863.

A creepy souvenir of this fight lies on a little table in the *Salle d'honneur*—an embalmed human hand. It is the hand of Captain Danjou, who was in command of a detachment of sixty men from the third company of the Legion who were killed to a man at Camaron. Over two thousand Mexican irregulars set upon the detachment in the neighbourhood of the village of Camaron. The detachment fought its way through the hostile cavalry to a farmhouse, entrenched itself there, and held out for a whole day against the overwhelming odds.

Five times were they called upon to surrender, and five times was the answer—"*Merde!*"

When the Mexicans at last took the house by storm, they found heaped up before the door a pile of dead. The few survivors were badly wounded. A few hours later relief came. But the French troops only found a heap of dead. Beside the captain's body lay his severed hand.

Weapons from all countries adorned the walls of the *Salle d'honneur*. Straight Mexican swords and curved Arabian *scimitars* of pliant steel hung side by side; beside poisoned arrows from Madagascar there were old-fashioned bayonets which had done all sorts of bloody work in the Legion's service. In the *Salle d'honneur* there are souvenirs of almost a century of battles.

The Foreign Legion was founded in the year 1831 under the name of "The African Auxiliaries."

The continual fighting in Algeria used to decimate the French troops posted there. In the reign of King Louis Philippe the idea was started of reviving the mediaeval institution of mercenaries, and of raising troops for service in Africa composed entirely of foreign adventurers. A Belgian adventurer who called himself Baron de Boegard, with no particular authority, but still without active opposition on the part of the King's generals, collected around him a band composed of the doubtful characters of all nations. He assumed the title of lieutenant-general, and finally succeeded in persuading the military authorities that his fellows would make capital stuff for service in Algeria.

About 4000 men took the oath of allegiance on the French colours in Marseilles and embarked for Africa. The French troops there turned up their noses at these tattered soldiers, and the hostile Arabs called them mockingly "the Bedouins from France,"[1] because they were so poor and ragged. The new-comers, however, plundered with such voracity as to astonish even the French troops, who were anything but scrupulous, and they were capital fighters into the bargain. A royal edict, dated March 10, 1831, sanctioned their incorporation in a Foreign Legion of their own under the name of the *Legion Etrangère*, on the pattern of the *Légion d'Hohenlohe*, which fought at the time of the Restoration. The regiment consisted of seven battalions, divided according to the different nationalities of the men:

1st, 2nd, and 3rd battalions   Swiss and Germans.

---

1. The Arabs who had established themselves in the towns used to despise the vagabond Bedouins.

4th battalion	Spaniards.
5th battalion	Italians.
6th battalion	Belgians and Dutchmen.
7th battalion	Poles.

After a short time the authorities left off separating the various nationalities from each other and contented themselves with teaching the foreigners the French words of command as quickly as possible.

A period of fighting now began for the Legion such as no regiment in the world has ever experienced.

Even in its first fights in Algeria the regiment suffered heavy losses. Then the King of France lent the Foreign Legion to the Queen Regent Christina of Spain to fight against the Carlists. For their services in Spain the Legion was to have been given 800,000 *francs*, but this sum was never paid. On the other hand, 3500 of the 4000 *légionnaires* fell in action. A bare 500 returned to Africa half starved and in rags.

New recruits joined—there has never been a lack of men ready to serve in the Foreign Legion. Algeria was conquered after ceaseless fighting, in which the battles of Condiat-Ati, M'Shomesh, Constantine, and Zaatcha were only the more important fights in an endless campaign. Even at this period of its existence the Legion grasped the fact that its mission was not only to furnish soldiers, but also pioneers, labourers, and city-builders.

They worked hard, building town after town, and there is today(at time of first publication), no city in French Northern Africa in which the first European building was not built by *légionnaires*. In the Crimean War the Legion was ordered to Russia, where, in the Battle of the Alma, it was the first regiment to come under fire and fought with great bravery. In General Canrobert's despatches 29 officers and men of the Legion were mentioned for bravery in the Battles of the Alma and Inkerman. In the siege of Sebastopol the Foreign Legion was very much to the fore and was cordially hated by the Russians. The besieged called them "the leather-bellies," from the great African cartridge-pouches which they wore in front. In the Crimea their losses were enormous, and Napoleon III. rewarded their services by naturalising a number of the Legion's officers and men.

At that time the Legion never experienced years of peace, only months of peace at the most, and even these were few and far between. *Les étrangers* were hardly home from the Crimea when a rebellion among the Algerian Arabs broke out, which led to the famous Arab expedition. The mighty Battle of Ischeriden brought the tribes of Beni Jenni, Beni Raten, and the Beni Amer into subjection. The regiment had a few hundred more to add to its list of dead and had won new honours, only, as a real regiment of mercenaries, to be transferred to a new field of battle. Real wandering Ahasvers were these African mercenaries. This time it was to Italy, to Magenta, that they were ordered. Again they came back, their numbers diminished by a thousand or more, and had to start once more from Sidi-bel-Abbès on an expedition against the natives in Morocco.

Thus passed the year 1860. During the next two years the Legion was engaged in desultory fighting against the Arabs and Bedouins without, to their great disgust, bringing off any *grande affaire*.

In February the Legion embarked for Mexico and witnessed the disastrous events of the short imperial period. They made roads, working hard, and occasionally brought off some mad exploit with the greatest bravery, adding that day at Camaron to the Legion's roll of honours. The result of the Mexican campaign, as far as the Legion is concerned, is best shown by their losses: 1918 men dead and missing; 328 died of their wounds; and 1859 met their deaths from various illnesses.

On coming back to Algeria the Legion filled up its ranks once more and was scattered in little detachments over the province of Oran to play, for the sake of variety, the part of settlers, digging wells, building villages, and laying roads—till the year 1870. In the Franco-German War the Legion first came into action at Orleans. All the German *légionnaires* had, however, been left in Africa. After the conclusion of peace the Legion helped in the putting down of the Commune, where so much blood was shed, and made itself thoroughly hated in Paris.

As had been the case since the foundation of the Legion, fights in Algeria began once more. The rebellion of the Kaid Si Hamze, in the year 1871 and the years following, brought them fresh campaigns. While de Négrier was colonel of the regiment he mounted a part of the Legion on mules, to be able to cover greater stretches of country, a system which has been kept up to this day, and which formed one of the first examples of mounted infantry. Till the year 1883 the *légionnaires* remained in Africa, and enjoyed a period of comparative quietude, which only brought a few Arab rebellions and a few dozen skirmishes.

Then, however, they started off once more on their travels. The Far East, Tonquin, was the scene of a colonial war against a brave enemy and a murderous climate. The victories of Bac-Ninh, Hong-Hoa, Soc-Nam, and Chu are so many days of fame for these foreign mercenaries, whose regimental history during these fifty years will never meet its equal. In the year 1892 we find the Legion in Dahomey fighting against King Behanzin, in the year 1895 in Madagascar. At the present date we hear of the regiment chiefly in Morocco.

This is merely a short sketch, a skeleton outline of the Legion's history—one of the most notable histories that any soldiers' chronicler can point to, the story of a band of homeless adventurers. Their pay was always ridiculously small, their punishments barbarous, and the discipline that they were subject to more than hard. And yet there were always thousands of recruits willing to shed their life's blood, who did not serve under the Legion's flag merely to earn their living, but formed one of the best bodies of troops in the world.

What misery and misfortune must there be in Europe to bring thousands and thousands of poor and desperate men flocking to the Legion's standard, whose total in the eighty years of the regiment's existence must add up to an overwhelming figure. I have been through all the French books on the Legion to try and find the exact figure, but without success. The exact strength of the Legion has always been kept well to the background. The two regiments have now and then reached an enormous strength. Beauvoir, for instance, mentions that in the year 1895 a single company in Sidi-bel-Abbès was 4864 men strong.

He gives the nationalities of the Legion in that year as follows:

Alsatians	45	*per cent.*
Germans	12	"
Swiss	8	"
Belgians	7	"
Frenchmen	5	"
Spaniards	5	"
Italians	5	"
Austrians	4	"
Dutchmen	4	"
From various countries	5	"

The average strength of the two battalions varies between 8000 and 12,000 men. The percentage of deaths from illness, above all fever, is extraordinarily high, and when to this we add the many thousands killed in battle, and consider that desertions are very frequent, we come to the astounding conclusion that in eighty years a good deal over a hundred thousand men have served under the Legion's flag.

In giving this figure I make no claim to accuracy. It may be far below the mark or again it may be a few thousands too high.

Be that as it may, a mighty army of men of all nations has served in the Foreign Legion, working hard and suffering the most awful hardships under an iron discipline that punishes even the most trivial offences with the hardest of punishments. The pay has never been higher than it is now; not enough to purchase even the trifles which a soldier needs to clean his uniform and equipment, to say nothing about his personal needs, be they ever so small. The assertion that these hundred thousand men have made the French Government a present of their work and strength during all these years, and all too often of their lives, is no exaggeration. Even though the history of the Foreign Legion, the history of that ever-fighting band of men, reads like a romance of mediaeval times, one is easily led to look at the matter from the French standpoint and to make the pharisaical assertion so commonly believed in France, that the Foreign Legion is the scum of humanity, useless human rubbish which has been turned into useful dung for colonisation, if one may use the expression, in the service of improvement.

The modern thinker is much more inclined to ask himself in wonderment how it came that year after year so many men were willing to sell their lives for a country that was not their own. These thousands have not even had the inducement of high wages.

Here we stand before a riddle, before some mysterious force which convinced these thousands of desperate men that the African Foreign Legion was their last refuge. The mighty deeds of the Legion are still more of a riddle. All these men have been clever enough to discover sooner or later what a very poor sort of bargain they made when they enlisted, and the Legion has always been a hotbed of seething discontent. As it is today, (at time of first publication), so has it always been; the only subject of conversation in the Legion is an endless discussion of that all-important question: how and when to desert. The *légionnaire* has enriched the French language with a variety of strange curses to give expression to his rage at the tyranny and infamous treatment of which he is the victim. It is really a marvel that these discontented fellows, soldiers who were always on the eve of deserting, always forgot their grievances when they came under fire.

One or two were perhaps men of the type which frequently occurs in the Legion of today, (at time of first publication), who only enlist to meet death in a form which appeals to their fancy, and who volunteer for one dangerous expedition after another till they meet the bullet for which they are so eager. But these have always been the exceptions. To the others fighting has always been a delight.

A detachment of men are stationed in an isolated fort. The heat of the sun is merciless, the hard work unbearable and the monotony of duty gets on their nerves: the whole garrison becomes restless and can only be kept in order with the greatest difficulty. Then comes the command to turn out: there is a prospect of soldiering in earnest: the men are beside themselves with joy—when they have to fight they are relieved from slavery.

This enthusiasm and passion to get at the enemy is the redeeming feature of many a ruined life. It acts as a safety-valve: otherwise the men could never stand the deadly monotony of their lives.

The soldiers of the Legion have never yet fought just because they had to fight, or because their officers urged them on to it or because they had to defend their own wretched lives. The history of the regiment can only tell of glorious attacks, of furious charges made with a bravery that absolutely disregards danger and death. These poor adventurers have their own individual ideas of honour for which they are proud to give their lives and which the only French general who ever understood the Legion expressed in a few enthusiastic words. It was General de Négrier who said:

Some soldiers can fight the légionnaire can die.

That is the *légionnaire*'s idea of honour: his own individual idea. He will never hear the signal for retreat. I have so often heard the murmur of discontent which runs through the ranks when the hated call is heard at a manoeuvre. Eleven times in its history has the Legion refused to obey when the signal for retreat was blown.

In France the performances of the Foreign Legion have always been recognised. It is true that the recognition has taken no substantial form. Its officers have always reaped the reward of quick promotion, but the *légionnaire* himself has always remained a poor devil without pay and without the slightest hope for the future.

Five *centimes* daily wages!

On paper the *légionnaire* is paid seven *centimes* a day. That's what stands in the French army list. Two *centimes* daily are, however, deducted for messing, so that the real wages are five *centimes per diem*. After the *second conge*, when he has five years' service behind him, his wages are raised to ten *centimes* daily; a corporal gets twenty *centimes*—a scale of pay which has perhaps a parallel in the Chinese army, certainly nowhere else in the world.

As a set-off against this miserable payment the French books on the subject draw attention to the chance of quick advancement. This, however, is a trifle contradictory to the actual facts of the case. In the Foreign Legion at present among a round three hundred officers there is only one who is not a Frenchman, a quondam officer in the Austrian army, who worked his way up from the ranks. Even among the non-commissioned officers the percentage of foreigners is very small. It can easily be understood that the colonel lays some stress on the fact that the non-coms shall be Frenchmen: this, however, renders the prospect of promotion for a foreigner proportionately small.

It is only now and again that a foreigner rises further than the rank of corporal. When he is specially talented he may become a sergeant but hardly ever reaches the rank of colour-sergeant. An exception to this rule is made in the case of officers who have been turned out of other armies. For these, the Foreign Legion has special regulations. They are not asked to show any papers nor are inquiries made into the reasons why they were originally dismissed: all that is required is a photograph showing him in uniform. They are then let off all recruits' work and are sent to the *peloton des élèves caporaux*, the non-commissioned officers' school, are in eight weeks corporal, and in four months sergeant. It is, however, a great rarity when one of these men rises any further.

Often enough one hears that the Legion's pension is a liberal one. The Legion has a right to a pension after fifteen years of service, and then he gets 500 *francs* a year. That sounds very fine. The fact, however, remains that a man who spends fifteen years in all sorts of climates, and who works for fifteen years with the energy required of a *légionnaire*, can easily amass a small fortune. Another interesting fact is that very few *légionnaires* are capable of serving fifteen years. They die long before the time is up: either from fever, overwork, or an enemy's bullet. . . . No, the Legion's pension system is a mockery.

The only sort of compensation that remains is the Cross of the Legion of Honour and the *Médaille militaire*, with both of which goes a sum of money; in the case of the Cross of the Legion of Honour a very considerable one. These distinctions, however, are so seldom conferred that they can hardly be taken into the question as representing a complement to the miserable pay, or as a possibility of earning anything other than coppers in the Legion.

The only tangible reward that those heroes, to whose deeds of honour the Hall of Honour bears witness, have earned has been:

Five *centimes* a day—those glorious days included.

And what is the end of it all? The *légionnaire's* life in the Legion begins with the motto, "*Work without pay*," and at the end of it he stands in the street like a beggar, and does not know what in the world to do for a living. Even in the rare cases in which the climate and the hardships he has undergone have not ruined his constitution, and his health is still good, he is quite helpless.

I have spoken with hundreds and thousands of these *légionnaires* who have served their time as they lounged about the courtyard of the barracks in Sidi-bel-Abbès, rejoicing that they had done with the Foreign Legion forever. They were dressed in a dark blue suit, which is served out from the quartermaster's office to those who have served their time, being made of an ugly blue stuff, which looks like blue sacking. Of course their clothes did not fit them in the least, the trousers being either too long or too short, and the coat looked like a sack, for how could one expect them to take any trouble about a good fit in the quartermaster's office. As head-gear they wore an enormous flat cap, such as the sailors in the ports on the Mediterranean wear. This suit, together with boots, a single pair of socks and a shirt, was all that they possessed after five years of service.

They had also the right of travelling free of charge to any town in France, and were given a *franc* a day as long as their journey lasted. No *légionnaire*, however, is transported to his real home, which is generally outside France. The majority, with grim humour, chose some town in the far north, generally Dunkirk, in order that the journey might be as long as possible. As a result of this the Mayor of Dunkirk wrote and begged the French Minister of War not to send any more *légionnaires* there. The authorities had not the faintest idea what to do with them; in Dunkirk there was not even enough work for the townsmen themselves.

A *légionnaire* who has served his time is thus absolutely helpless, being stranded penniless in a totally strange town. His clothes are such as to prevent him applying for any work but that of a labourer, and the only papers he has to show are his certificates of dismissal from the Foreign Legion, which are worth very little in France. There are plenty of fine speeches made about the glorious Foreign Legion in the French Republic, but there is a prejudice against having anything to do with a *légionnaire* in the flesh there. Everywhere he is shown the door, and the poor devil begins a terrible course of starvation.

How often have I seen these men come back again with a batch of recruits to Sidi-bel-Abbès, and their old comrades mockingly asking them why they were in Africa once more. It was always the same old story: for days and weeks and even months starving and half perished with cold they had struggled against their fate, and gone from house to house seeking work until their clothes were mere rags and their boots were worn out. Finally, they had despaired of ever finding work, and had begun to *coquet* with the thought that in the Legion they had at least had enough to eat, with the result that in a few days they had sought out the nearest recruiting-office, and had bound themselves for a further five years of slavery.

This after five long years of work—the gratitude of France.

CHAPTER 9

"March or Die!"

Weeks passed. Recruit time was over, and I was serving with the troops.

From the very beginning I was anxious to do my duty as well as I could. The real soldier's duties were a pleasure to me, and like the other *légionnaires* who daily debated the chances of receiving marching orders, I longed with fantastical impatience for active service.

The Legion always seemed to me to be in a state of feverish impatience, always on the jump, always expecting marching orders. The regiment's traditional fiery military spirit infected even the youngest recruits. When vague rumours of a new rising of the Arabs on the Morocco frontier penetrated to the barracks, or when the *Echo d'Oran* with the laconic brevity of official telegrams announced new skirmishes in Indo-China, the news spread like wildfire through the Legion's quarters. Everywhere you could see groups of *légionnaires*, speaking of their hopes of at last receiving marching orders. When an especially exciting report had been spread, they sometimes stood in crowds before the regimental offices, waiting for one of the clerks to rush down the stairs with the news:

"*Faites le sac.*"

Pack your knapsacks! This is the old ominous war-cry that sounds from room to room when the Legion mobilises, the dry business-like password calling the Legion to its military business.

The thirst for adventure, which is an element of the Legion, as inseparable from it as poverty and hard work, always lay in the air.

For the first time I heard the alarm sounded in the middle of night. I jumped up out of my sleep in a fright. "*Aux armes!*" the bugle sounded from the barrack-yard. The sergeants and corporals rushed through the barracks crying the alarm, "*Aux armes!*"—To arms!

All at once the stillness of the night was turned into a perfect pandemonium—shouting and yelling and roaring sounded from room to room, the barracks were in an uproar.

"*Faites le sac. En tenue de campagne d'Afrique*," the corporals shouted, and renewed rejoicing answered them.

The "African field equipment *café*" was not such a simple thing, and in spite of all the yelling and shouting we worked with feverish excitement, for in ten minutes we had to stand in the barrack-yard ready for marching. There was singing and whistling everywhere while the knapsacks were packed and everybody wondered whether we were going "*au Maroc*" at last or whether the Arab tribes of the South were in rebellion again. The cartridge-cases were brought from the magazine and their covers burst open with hatchets. The packets of cartridges were thrown from man to man. We tore off the cardboard covering and . . . saw that they were blank cartridges.

"*Merde!*" roared Corporal Wassermann.

Roaring and singing stopped as if by magic. As blank cartridges only were served out, it could but be a question of a short manoeuvre and the Legion would not dream of working up enthusiasm for an ordinary "*marche militaire*." In this case the short manoeuvre march really extended over three hundred *kilometres* three hundred *kilometres* to the South,—three hundred *kilometres* back again; a total distance of six hundred *kilometres*, which is about four hundred miles. . . .

By the light of a lantern the companies formed up in the barrack-yard. In a moment the baggage and ammunition carts were packed, because the Legion always carries sharp ammunition on the march to be prepared for any emergency. Then we went out into the night to the tune of the Legion's march.

Anyone who has once heard the march of the Legion will never forget it, its peculiar sharp rhythm broken by the bugles' storm signal. The Legion's band is forbidden to play it in the garrison or on the parade—the regimental march is played before the enemy or on long marches.

Sidi-bel-Abbès woke up as soon as the band commenced to play in the quiet streets; windows were thrown open and out of the corners all the riff-raff of the sleeping town came into view: miserable-looking white men and dirty negroes looked at the marching company with sleepy eyes in high astonishment. In a few minutes we were out of town and marched along the yellow sandy road in dim moonlight. The marching order was in column of four as is customary in the

Legion.

I marched in the first row of fours of my company. In the front the four drummers plodded along close behind our captain's white horse. Abreast of the captain walked Lieutenant Garde-Jörgensen, a Dane, a soldier of fortune. . . .

The silent march into the night was trying for my burning curiosity, and I did a most unmilitary thing:

"Where are we going to, Lieutenant?" I asked.

The officer nearly burst with laughter.

"I don't know myself where we are going to," he said. "If you were an old *légionnaire* you would not ask, my boy. We are marching. We are probably marching for a long time. We are always marching. We never know if we are only going to manoeuvre or to meet the enemy. That's how it is. *Tiens!* will you have a cigarette?"

The first rows were laughing and Smith was shouting in his deep voice:

"*Le sac, ma foi, toujours au dos.*"

Renewed laughter. Everyone was talking and wondering where we were marching to and how long the march would last. Some of them thought it was nothing but a night march; others discussed the probability of "real work" being in sight.

"What do you think you know about it?" said Smith to me with a grin. "Nothing. We march, sonny, and that's all there is to do. God and the colonel know what's going to come of it."

We heard the clatter of a galloping horse and turning our heads curiously we saw a bright spot on the uniform of the rider, sparkling like a star. The rider was the Commander-General of Algeria, and the shining spot on his breast was the Grand Cross of the Legion of Honour.

"*Oh, la la,*" said Smith, shaking his head. "Tell you what, Dutchy, if the old man himself has got up in the middle of the night you may send your little legs a message to get ready for a lot of work. Now we shall march, sonny. You can bet your bottom dollar on that. The old man there means manoeuvring, heaps of it, or—Arabs."

Milestone after milestone passed by and the jokes ceased very soon, as the marching regiment settled down to business. Silently the regiment tramped onwards. The knapsack pressed heavily; heads went down and shoulders bent low to spread the heavy weight on the back; the gun-straps cut into the shoulders until one's right arm was almost lame and the painful prickly feeling caused by the non-circulating blood had grown permanent.

After the first ten *kilometres* a shrill signal-whistle sounded and the whole company wheeled off to the roadside to rest in long line for five minutes. I pulled off my knapsack and threw it upon the ground with a feeling of relief, joyful at getting rid of the heavy weight for a few minutes. To my great astonishment, the other men kept their knapsacks on their backs and at once threw themselves at full length on the ground. Later on I did the same. The halt was so short that one lost priceless seconds in taking off and strapping on the knapsack, seconds only, but even seconds are precious for the marching *légionnaire*.

Five minutes is but a short span of time. But never in my life has a time of rest seemed so delicious, so beneficial, so reviving as when I lay stretched out on the hot African sand for those pitifully short five minutes. . . .

The company wheeled into column again and trudged forwards on the endless road, whose straight sameness was only interrupted by the mile-stones. With each mile it became quieter in the marching rows. The legs and back were strained to the utmost, and a word spoken appeared a waste of energy. One seemed to be a machine, marching on mechanically behind the man in front when once put in motion; each man was sufficiently occupied with himself. If anyone in utter weariness took a step to the right or a step to the left out of marching line, he got an oath hurled at him—you were so tired that even the slight touch of your comrade swaying out of line was an extra burden to the tormented body.

When the morning mists and the bitter cold of the dawn were followed by the hot burning sun, we had accomplished a march of forty *kilometres*, and the time came when our legs refused to do any more. When the signal sounded for rest, we fell down helpless, and when we started marching again, it looked as if a crowd of invalids and old men were slowly wandering down the road. The worn-out legs revenged themselves for the hard usage they had received. During the halt the flow of blood was hemmed in the limbs. Standing on one's feet again, one felt a sharp stinging pain in the soles. Every step was torture. For five minutes afterwards one crawled along as best one could, till one became once more an unfeeling automaton.

Again the slow progress past the milestones. At eleven o'clock in the morning we reached a little village. The marks on the last milestone said that we were fifty *kilometres* from Sidi-bel-Abbès. We passed by the old rickety houses of the village, and at a given signal the regiment halted, the companies forming up on the dry, sandy piece of ground to the left of the street.

Then followed the command: "Halt!" and immediately afterwards the order: "*Campez!*"

In a moment we had piled our arms. The knapsacks were thrown to the ground and the folding tent-supports and the tent-covers pulled out. Then the corporal of each section stepped out of the line, holding the tent-poles high above his head to mark the tent line for the whole company. Again a short command, and in a few seconds the waste surface of sand was covered with little white tents.

It was a miracle. We were so well drilled and each individual knew his part so well that it only took a few seconds to pitch a tent. With surprising quickness the long rows of soldiers were turned into a tent encampment and five minutes afterwards the officers' tents were pitched in a final row. In the meantime *Madame la Cantinière* had hauled out of her sutler's cart folding tables and benches, ready to do a roaring trade with the tired-out *légionnaires*. The heavy Algerian wine was indeed a blessing after such a march and the poor devil who in these marching days did not possess a few coppers felt poor indeed.

In ten minutes the narrow trenches for cooking were dug out and in twenty places camp fires flared up simultaneously. The patrol marched round and round the white "soldiers' city." The food, consisting of macaroni and tinned meat, was greedily devoured.

After this the quiet of utter exhaustion reigned in the camp. The *légionnaires* lay huddled together in the tiny tents, on blankets spread out on the ground, covered with their cloaks, while the knapsacks served for a pillow. The rifles were brought into the tents and tied firmly together with a long chain by the corporal of each squad, who fastened the end of the chain to his wrist as a further precaution, for the Arabs had a habit of creeping through the lines on a dark night and stealing the much-coveted weapons from the tents. The patrols of the Legion have standing orders to challenge an Arab only once at night and then to fire. Even in this first night the watch caught a thief. The Arab was badly treated and he was delivered up to the civil authorities in the village the next morning in a horrible condition.

By seven o'clock in the evening the whole camp was fast asleep, sleeping the sleep of exhaustion.

An hour after midnight, in the flittering light of a magnificent starry sky, the companies formed up and continued the route to the South. This march lasted eight days. On one day the troops covered forty *kilometres*, making up the average again the next day with fifty *kilometres*. The monotony of this march and the physical strength and endurance it claimed of each of us cannot be described. At last, at the beginning of the real desert, we depended on the oasis-wells with their poor supply of water to quench our thirst, and the want of water was added to our sufferings.

At night, when starting on the march, the field-flasks were filled. The distribution of water was conducted under sharp supervision. Every man got two litres of dirty, muddy water. Company orders warned us to save up half a litre for the morrow's *soupe*. On camping next day every *légionnaire* had to give up half a litre of water to the mess of his company for cooking purposes. Whoever had emptied his field-flask during the heat and weariness of the march and was unable to deliver any water only got a handful of raw rice given him; he had to get it cooked as best he could.

This is one of the many brutal rules in force on these marches and there is method in it. Contrary to most of the *légionnaires*, I have always seen the necessity for the hard marching discipline. Troops that have to march in such droughty country must be able to economise their water rations. This is simply a law of necessity. There is another brutal feature of the Legion's marches: cruel at first sight but it is really kindness to the men. A *légionnaire* who faints on the march is tied to the baggage-cart. A pole is pushed through the sides of the cart at about the height of a man's arms and the *légionnaire* roped to it by the shoulders. The pole keeps him in a standing position—the cart rolls on. He either has to march or he is dragged along the uneven ground.

Seeing the thing done for the first time, I was filled with indignation at the apparent brutality of this torture. But afterwards I understood. In the wars in the South the fighting value of the Foreign Legion depends solely on its marching capability. Very often the ambulance is not able to follow. If the *légionnaire* remains behind the company in the desert, if only a *kilometre*, he is irretrievably lost. Hundreds and hundreds of men incapable of marching have found a terrible end in this way. The Arab women, who are far more cruel than the men, soon surround the helpless man, who suffers a painful death, after being horribly mutilated and disfigured.

Separation from the troops means death. This was not only the case at the time of the great Arab mutiny, which affected the whole of Algeria, but is the same today. Peace between the French and the Arabs down in the far south of Algeria is a myth. At the small military stations on the borders of the Sahara little skirmishes are a daily occurrence. When the station is alarmed and the thirty or forty men garrisoned there set out to pursue the pillaging Bedouin tribes, every *légionnaire* knows well that now he must march, or if he cannot march any more, he must die. March or die!

Death at the hands of Arab women! The *légionnaire* does not count the Bedouin or the Arab as a personal enemy; he is rather grateful to the robber of the desert for being the cause of a little change and excitement in the terribly monotonous life on the border stations. But upon the Arab woman the old *légionnaire* looks as upon a devil. He thinks of the hellish tortures that wounded men have suffered at the hands of Arab women, he remembers the mutilated bodies of *légionnaires* who had died an awful death after being tortured for many hours.

In the fourth year of his service, Rassedin had been ordered to one of the little Sahara stations, where he had seen much of the cruelty of the Arab women. Once a scouting party of his detachment found a skeleton in the sand of the desert. Shreds of a uniform showed that the skeleton had once been a soldier of the Legion. The skeleton's head was lying between the legs. . . . Another time the corporal of Rassedin's squad was missed at the morning call. In the evening he had taken a walk just in the neighbourhood of the station and had not returned. After a short search they found him.

"He was dead. But even in death I could see the frightful agony in his wide-open eyes," Rassedin declared. "Both legs were broken and bent backwards. The lower part of his body was slashed to pieces, but none of his wounds was deadly. They must have tormented him for hours. From that time we made no difference between men and women in fighting, but shot down every one. How did we know that it had really been women who had tortured the corporal? The dead man clutched a piece of a glass bracelet in his hand, which he must have torn off the arm of his tormentor in the struggle. Such bangles are only worn by the Bedouin women."

That is the reason why the *légionnaire* has come to look upon the Arab woman as the incarnation of the Devil. I have already recorded the story of the soldier with the skull tattooed on his forehead, who showed me a tobacco-pouch made out of a woman's breast.

As an example of unnecessary, quite unjustifiable brutality I will tell you what I had to suffer personally during the manoeuvre march. Whether freezing under the thin blanket in the cold icy nights in that climate of quickly changing temperatures was the cause, or the bad water, or the physical over-exertion of the marches, at any rate I suffered from tormenting pains in the stomach. Every few minutes during the march I got cramps and could only painfully drag myself along, doubled up like a worm. When we got to camp my strength was done. I went to the doctor's tent accompanied by the *caporal du jour* with the sick list. The doctor, an army surgeon, whose name I unfortunately have forgotten, pulled the book angrily out of the corporal's hand, and roared at him:

"On the march there are no sick men. Your company ought to know that."

The corporal shrugged his shoulders. "By order of the captain!" he said laconically.

Now the doctor turned to me.

"What's wrong?"

I briefly described the cramps in my stomach, and emphasised that I only wished to ask for something to relieve the pain, an opiate, perhaps, and that I intended to continue my duties.

He looked at me for a moment, and then said contemptuously:

"What do you know about opiates? To judge from your accent you are an Englishman."

"No, *monsieur le docteur*, a German."

"Well, I will tell you something. We know these little tricks. All the same if you're English, German or Hottentot, I take you to be quite a common simulator. I shall give you a certificate of being *non-malade*—not sick. *Non-malade*, corporal."

I was crushed. Astonishment fought with anger. At the very moment when the doctor was speaking to me I was almost doubled up with pain. "Not sick" That meant not only the loss of an opiate, but also heavy punishment. Anyone who is declared by the doctor as "not sick" is at once held guilty of simulation, and punished with the usual four days' imprisonment.

I saluted and said:

"*Non-malade, monsieur le docteur?* Without any examination?"

"*Va-t-en!*" roared the surgeon. "Get out of this."

The corporal shook his head as we went through the camp, and advised me to be patient. He believed that I was in pain, and he knew that that "pig of a doctor" had already sent many a man to his doom. But a complaint would only make matters worse, he said. I did not answer and thought of the coming night. I should be tied to a peg in front of the watch-tent, and would be. obliged to lie on the bare ground in the icy cold without any covering because I had been imprudent enough to ask for a little medicine. Maddening anger arose within me. When the corporal had made his report, my captain sent for me:

"You have not been punished so far?"

"No."

"What is the reason of your simulating?"

Then I lost control over myself, and in a fit of excitement hurled reproaches and accusations at the officer. The doctor was a fool and a disgrace to his profession. His diagnosis was an infamous and deliberate lie, and it was a disgrace that such people held authority. I do not remember everything I yelled out then, but it was a nice collection of the choicest epithets—rank insubordination! At length my attack of mad fury ended with my demanding to be taken before the commander of the regiment, and I threatened (this must have been very ridiculous) to complain to the French Minister of War.

The captain listened to me quietly and said:

"I believe that you have been badly treated. I will write a letter for you to the assistant surgeon, who will give you medicine. I should not advise you to send in a complaint to the regiment."

Then after a pause:

"What do you really expect? What do you want? We are in the Legion. You are a *légionnaire*—don't forget that again, *légionnaire!*"

If I had not in my complete loss of self-control ventured to air my opinions in language unheard of in the Legion, I should very likely have left the ominous peg in front of the guard-tent as a dead man.

Thanks to the opium pills of the assistant surgeon I was able, however, to march the next day with the others, but not without exerting every spark of my will-power. The time from one milestone to the other seemed endless. The expectation of the five minutes' rest at the fifth milestone was the power that drove me forward. I counted my steps in order to make me forget the pain in the mechanical occupation of counting. One hundred and twenty steps represented one hundred metres; when I had counted ten times one hundred and twenty, we had covered a *kilometre*, the fifth part of the road to rest. . . .

At last we reached our paradise, the few minutes of exhausted rest. And then the torment began afresh. . . .

The manoeuvres in a desert covered with peculiarly sharp stones, three hundred *kilometres* south of Sidi-bel-Abbès, occupied exactly eight hours, and from the standpoint of the Legion they were super-fluous and consequently useless. The development of the firing-line, the skilled search for cover, the rush of the bayonet attack, the under-standing of all the orders, the complete discipline under fire, are things which, in the never-ending practical military training of this fighting regiment, become part and parcel of the *légionnaire's* flesh and blood.

The closing manoeuvre was (I heard our captain discussing these matters with Lieutenant Garde) nothing more than a small private entertainment on the part of our colonel, who wished to show off with his regiment; a military amateur dramatic performance. On the other hand, the commander-general had said to his adjutant that it was a great pleasure to him to give his *légionnaires* an "airing." The regiment had already idled about barracks for six months, and might in the end forget that its real home was amongst the sand of the desert, and that it had no other object in life than to march, march a lot, to go on marching.

The *légionnaires* knew this fad of the general's well enough, and never called him anything else but the "marching pig." The fat ser-geant of our first *peloton* used to say, with great lack of respect:

"As soon as I see the fellow I feel tired. . . ."

When the general was still colonel and in command of the first regiment, he once met a drunken *légionnaire* in one of the side streets of Sidi-bel-Abbès. The man, only just capable of saluting, got the mad idea to address his colonel.

"*Eh, mon colonel,*" he stammered, "I am still very thirsty. Ten *sous, mon colonel.*" The colonel treated him to a stony stare. This look out of the hard eyes turned the *légionnaire* sober in a moment, and a brilliant idea struck him.

"You know I am the best marcher in my company, *mon colonel.*"

At this the colonel smiled and gave him a five-*franc* piece.

It is these little anecdotes and the rough jokes in the jargon of the Legion that are typical of the great weight laid on the marching performances in the Foreign Legion, without regard to the wear and tear of the human machine, without consideration of the many lives that are lost.

Even General de Négrier, the only commander that the Legion loved because he loved the Legion and knew how to come into per-sonal touch with each *légionnaire*, knew no mercy in the matter of marching. When he was commander of the Foreign Legion he did everything in his power for his troops. Each *légionnaire* was allowed to come to him with his personal affairs, every wounded man was a hero in his eyes, a brave man, for whom he could not do enough. But when he saw an exhausted *légionnaire* stumble out of the ranks and collapse during the terrible marches in Madagascar, the expression in his face became hard and pitiless. That was a grievous crime in his eyes. Then he would cry out the three words that have since become a proverb of the Legion:

"*March or die!*"

Marches which no European commander would attempt are nothing out of the common; they are the basis on which the Foreign Legion has won its laurels. But they are also the foundation for illness, decline, and death.

In each of these marches is embodied the principle of absolute disregard for human life. The possibility of such disregard is one of the chief advantages of the Foreign Legion in the eyes of the authorities. From a military point of view the marches of the Legion are splendid, a triumph of training and discipline; from a humane standpoint they are the height of unprincipled exploitation. No New York Jewish clothes-dealer, who keeps hundreds of people at starvation wages at the sewing-machines, does such a splendid piece of business as *la Légion*, which for a mere nothing saps the life from thousands of human creatures. It is not the cruelties of the penal battalion, not the brutality of punishments, not the poor devils who for some mere trifle are shot under martial law, that illustrate best the horrors of the Legion system. It is the marches that do this; the marches of the Foreign Legion condemn the system of the Foreign Legion!

Our manoeuvre march of 600 *kilometres* occupied sixteen days. On the stages in the far south the rations consisted almost entirely of rice, and to the hardships of the daily 40 *kilometres* the pangs of hunger were added. In spite of that the distance daily covered remained the same.

I still suffered from pains in my stomach. Today it is a puzzle to me how I managed to march 300 *kilometres* in this condition in the burning sun and to stand the cold during the nights. But others were no better off. They marched with open wounds in their feet; with blisters between neck and shoulder-blades, where the straps of the heavy knapsack pressed; with eyes inflamed by the sun; with severe bronchial troubles; with bleeding and festering sores on their thighs. Many limped, and most marched bent well-nigh double, sunk together—a miserable, pitiful sight. Surly, silent, raging bitterness pictured in the hard lines of the face and in the tired eyes, we stamped onwards. The only words heard were curses.

Our nerves were strained to bursting-point. Over the whole troop lay the strain of over-exertion, bodily and mental nerve-sickness. The Foreign Legion has manufactured a special expression of its own for this mental state—"*Cafard.*"

The *cafard* reigned. The *cafard* of the Foreign Legion, a near relative to tropical madness, is a collective name for all the inconceivable stupidities, excesses and crimes which tormented nerves can commit. The English language has no word for this condition. In *cafard* murder hides, and suicide and mutiny; it means self-mutilation and planless flight out into the desert; it is the height of madness and the depth of despair. Many nights we were roused from sleep by a pandemonium of noise. *Légionnaires*—*légionnaires* in *cafard*—jumped round the tents in the dim light of the watch-fires, roaring the old Legion song out into the night. The "song" commenced with abusing the corporal and went on through the whole scale of charges up to the commander-general—in a horrible Legion French, of which the chief advantage was its extraordinary power of detailed expression. No officer was passed over in this song and each one was carefully mentioned by name, so that there might be no mistake. . . .

The song was painted with insults in rainbow colours. The insinuation that Captain So-and-So kept up his private *harem* with the funds of the company was one of the most harmless, and with the assertion that he was an old monkey, the register of the regiment commander's sins only began.

At the top of their voices the *cafard* madmen shrieked this song of insubordination out into the still night, until the camp became lively. With many oaths the sentries tussled with the mad singers, and from out of the darkness bawling voices roared applause.

Such things were not taken seriously. The "singers" were bound to pegs in front of the guard-tent over the night, to give them a chance to cool down, and they had to join their companies at daybreak—to march on.

When we got back to Sidi-bel-Abbès, our uniforms and our spirits were in sad condition. . . .

Chapter 10

The Madness of the Foreign Legion

In the interval between the terrible exertions of the great manoeuvre march and a period of hard work in the sewers of the Arab prison of Sidi-bel-Abbès, something I had long been dreading occurred. Even by changing my few gold pieces into the smallest of coppers, I could not spin them out eternally. One fine day the sum of my riches consisted of three thick, round copper pieces. Although big and heavy, they were not worth more than a few cents.

I lay stretched out on my bed, tired and vexed Smith, who, being a bugler, was not obliged to waste his strength in cleaning Arab sewers, was chaffing me. He thought it a great joke to inquire with friendly solicitude about the unpleasant details of my work.

I did not like his raillery. Wishing for revenge I remembered with grim humour that the state of my finances would be of a certain interest to my friend Smith.

"Hallo, bugler," said I.

Smith, lounging on his bed, muttered something about privileged sons of the Prophet—and inquired if the Arab convicts had been satisfied with my work?

"Bugler, I've no more money!" I said.

He jumped up from his bed, looking at me aghast.

"What d'you say?"

"My money is finished."

Smith's face grew long.

He was evidently thinking of the countless casks of wine lying stored in Sidi-bel-Abbès. . . . All at once his face cleared. He had found a way out of the difficulty.

"Send for some more!" he advised.

I shook my head.

"Nonsense," said the bugler, with the happy confidence of the Legion. "They'll send you some, a *légionnaire* always gets something sent him. Shall I help you to write a real, nice, touching letter, Dutchy?"

Again I shook my head. But the bugler would not let me off so easily. Going through the different grades of relationship, he inquired as to my connections. When I declared with intentional spitefulness that they were all as poor as church mice, he swore a little in Arabic and thoughtfully repeated a chapter of the *Koran*, treating of the duties of friendship. A little inspired by this, he asked for a whole hour about my former friends. I told him that they were either dead or on the point of starvation. The bugler thought this ridiculous, but with much tact did not continue the subject, coming, no doubt, to the conclusion that I had either killed somebody or robbed a bank in good old Germany. Nothing but that could keep a *légionnaire* from writing begging letters!

I let the philosopher keep his opinion.

After thinking deeply for a time, he muttered nothing but a resigned, "*C'est la Légion.*"

After a while he asked: "And is there really nothing left?"

Without saying a word, I pulled out my three copper pieces.

Then a slight smile spread over his face. "Do you know, we'll buy drink with that," he said softly. As we went down the stairs to the canteen, he wisely proposed buying two half-bottles instead of a whole one, for the half-bottles were always filled three-quarters full by *Madame la Cantinière*. In this way we got the fullest measure possible for the three coppers.

My friend the bugler emptied the bottle with great respect, till not a drop was left. Then he became sad again, but said in a comforting way:

"*Inschallah*—and if we haven't any money, sonny, then we've got none. But if I were you, I should after all write to somebody for a little brass—"

Only now, in my utter destitution, did I really recognise my position. The few pieces of silver I had still had in my possession, which in former times would just have been sufficient for a few theatre tickets or a few hundred cigarettes, had, in the land of Sidi-bel-Abbès, been a fortune, and had saved me from much wearisome, petty work. Thanks to them, I had been able, after long marches or heavy fatigue duty, to go straight into town without having to bother about polishing and washing. The smallest coin could purchase release from these burdens—now all this was at an end. For hours after I came off duty, I, like the others, stood at the wash-tub, or tediously polished my leather-work.

My horizon had narrowed; now it only encircled the drill-ground, barrack-yard, and my bunk in the Legion's quarters. I spent hours lying on my bed and staring at the whitewashed wall opposite, with the long shelf on which the knapsacks were packed. My interests were now quite taken up by all the petty, trifling considerations of the Legion. I quarrelled with the others whether it were really my turn to fetch fresh water in the big earthenware jug; I disputed the highly important matter of sweeping underneath my bed, and it was a question of vital interest to me whether I was ordered to scrub the bench or the large table at the great Saturday cleaning. . . . The bench was so much easier to do.

The days all passed in the same monotonous manner. The grey sameness tired the brain and made one indifferent to the little considerations and small services that people should render to each other when living such a hard life, crowded into so small a space. Everywhere the worst side of human nature showed itself, and even the greatest fool was soon clever enough to find out the bad points of the man who worked beside him by day and slept next to him at night. Petty malice, ill-natured gossip, ridiculous intrigues formed the atmosphere of the Legion.

I learnt to know a great deal about human nature, and what I learnt was not inspiriting. With the exception of jolly Herr von Rader, Abramovici was the only man I knew who had a spark of humour left in him. He was the queerest character in the room. He declared he was a Roumanian, but only spoke German, and that with a terrible Berlin accent, which was, to say the least, very strange in a Roumanian. When questioned as to his religion, he told the corporal that he was a "pork-eating" Jew. I suppose he meant that he had no delicate convictions.

The man was tall and very thin and appeared to be made of India-rubber. His long neck was surmounted by a head like that of a bird of prey, continually turning from side to side so as not to miss an opportunity of stealing something from his comrades. He had a vile mouth under his enormous nose. In a whining tone he swore all day long at providence in general and the Legion in particular. Nobody could resist his volubility and he was the first, the last, and the only *légionnaire* who ever succeeded in never doing any work.

The explanation of his French nickname, "*Viaïsse*," was that the India-rubber man repeated the Yiddish phrase of lament, "*Wie haisst!*" about ten times in one sentence. Once when he made a complaint about something or other to the captain, the latter had thrown up his hands in despair and called out, "*Viaïsse, viaïsse, sacré nom de Dieu! toujours viaïsse*—what does the fellow want?" The whole regiment laughed at "*Monsieur Viaïsse*"; he was never called by his real name, Abramovici, but officers and corporals called to him: "*Eh, Viaïsse*, come here! "He never worked. He was only saved from punishment by his inherent gift of humour. He was very tall, his arms nearly reaching to the ground. If one of his superiors ever ventured to give him any work to do, the scraggy "India-rubber man" appeared to personify a whole Ghetto. His eyes grew large and staring, the nose purple, and the head moved backwards and forwards like a pendulum.

Then *Viaïsse* took a deep breath, and a mad flow of words poured from his vile mouth, while the long arms, with the outspread claw-like fingers, waved frantically in the air.

". . . *Wie haisst! nom de Dieu, de bon Dieu de la Légion*—damn me, why should I work myself to death? I've had to drill the whole forenoon and have got *nix* to eat but a poor soup. I'm a stricken man and will have to get some extra food if I am not to fall down dead like a dog, you jewel of a sergeant. *Wie haisst!* I am a ruined man if I don't get some food at once. Well?"

It is impossible to repeat it all. Words fail me when I try to reproduce my friend Abramovici's grand flow of language. In one respect he was indeed a friend to me; no one ever made me laugh as much as he did. On the day of his arrival with the depot-train from Oran, I happened to hear when the sergeant of the company for the first time ordered him to do some work. Abramovici nearly got a fit at this unheard-of demand. His arms waved frantically in the air like a windmill, and wild words flowed from his mouth.

The poor sergeant wished to put in a word sideways. He wished to give a quiet command, he wanted to get furious. But he could not. He could only see with numb astonishment the lurid red nose, he turned away to get out of the reach of the "windmill arms," and at last fell down on the nearest bed with a horrible Arab oath, and laughed as he had never laughed before in his life. When he at last recovered his breath again, he said in broken German: "*Oh. Gott in Himmel, cet homme là, zu viel sprechen.*—Talks too much."

But Abramovici went on jabbering, until at last his harangue ended in laments to the God of his Fathers.

This was the way he always got off—one so seldom hears a laugh down there that *Monsieur Viaïsse* was highly appreciated by officers and men.

He called me his friend. He began our friendship with the conventional question:

"*Wie haisst!* will you give me a cigarette?"

Many a cigarette the Roumanian Jew from Berlin got from me, as long as there was silver in my pocket. In return he assured me of his high esteem, and when longing for a smoke called me "*Herr Baron.*" When with the silver pieces the cigarettes came to an end, our friendship suffered a little in consequence.

I myself lived in a state of continual irritation. The least trifle put me into such a rage that I can hardly credit it today. Often enough I would tear down my *paquetage* from the shelf, destroying what had been wearisome work, just because some trousers or jacket did not seem to be folded correctly. It had been nothing else but *cafard* when I had roared at the captain because the doctor refused to give me an opiate on the march—it was exactly the same *cafard* in a milder form when I roared at this or that comrade just because he was in my way when I was busy polishing. My vexation, my irritability, my brooding was the madness of the Foreign Legion.

No *légionnaire* escapes from it.

The rest of my comrades in the room all had at different times the *cafard* more or less seriously.... Crowded together like horses in a bad stable the men became dangerous. They fought over the quarter of a litre of the Legion wine that was apportioned to us every second day, and watched with ridiculous suspicion that the next man did not get more than he did; one quarrelled over a piece of bread; one took one's neighbour for a thief who wanted to steal a bit of black wax for leather polishing. If one man got more work to do than his neighbour, he cried murder and roared out about protection, and favouritism, and vicious preference.

This was the atmosphere in which the Legion whims were developed. It was really strange how many of the *légionnaires* had a screw loose, often only harmless peculiarities, but which could increase to madness.

All idiocy in the Legion is called *cafard*. A *légionnaire* is gloomy, sitting sullenly on his bed for hours, speaking to no one. If you ask him what is the matter, he will answer with a gross insult. He sits thinking all the time and does the queerest things. He has the *cafard*. . . .

His madness may turn into a senseless explosion or fit of fury; men suffering from *cafard* will run a bayonet through their comrade's body, without any reason, without any outward cause. Sometimes they rush out into the desert, sometimes they tear every piece of their outfit into rags, just to vex themselves and others thoroughly.

The *cafard* is at its worst in the hot season when the sun burns down relentlessly from the cloudless, deep blue sky, with the strange greenish colouring of the horizon peculiar to Algeria. Then the barrack-yard of the Foreign Legion lies deserted. It is so hot that the stones on the yellow clayey ground seem to move in the glimmering overheated air. The *légionnaire* sentries wear the flowing white neck-protector, and have stuffed wet cloths into their *kepis*.

In the soldiers' quarters the *légionnaires* lie on their mattresses and take their *siesta*, the strictly prescribed rest from 11 a.m. until 3 p.m. The white man is a useless object in the sun-blaze of the hot season. In the infernal heat of the soldiers' rooms the *cafard* has often been the cause of great disaster. It has often happened that during the *siesta légionnaires* have suddenly jumped out of the window, three stories high, without any outward cause whatever.

Once (very likely when affected with *cafard*) I wrote down during the *siesta* a description of what our men's room looked like. These few lines are the only thing I ever wrote in the Legion:

I lay on my bed half naked. The room was as hot as a stove, filled with the stench of perspiration. A brilliant strip of sunlight played through the long room from window to window. Oh, the heat, the heat. Even the walls felt hot. In the bare, whitewashed room the men lay groaning on their beds in all kinds of possible and impossible positions. Some were swearing, others quarrelling—nothing brings on the *cafard* so quickly as physical suffering. Two Spaniards were quarrelling in the loud gesticulating manner of their race; a German in the next bed had fallen asleep, and was muttering words of German in his dream. He was dreaming of his mother.

In the other corner of the room a Frenchman was shouting frantically to someone to give him a brush—his own brush was lost. His bed neighbour hummed a marching song, half in Arabic, half in French, always with the same refrain:

Si le caporal savait ça, il dirait: Nom de Dieu.

Another man slowly and automatically rubbed his leather

straps, a third one informed everybody that the sergeant was a rogue and was working him to death. Here the German awoke. Disturbed in his sleep he yelled out: 'Shut up you beggars.' And the Frenchmen and Spaniards began to curse on hearing German words.

'*Monsieur le Caporal*'[1] sat up slowly and tiredly and, leaning on his elbow, said in a low tone of voice:

'A little silence, please.'

The Spaniards laughed and a Frenchman said under his breath, the damned '*casque à pique*,' meaning the Prussian helmet, might leave honest *légionnaires* in peace during *siesta*.

The corporal did not move. In his quiet even tone he went on speaking: 'Silence. You all know that during *siesta* all noise is forbidden. Legrand, for using the epithet "*casque à pique*," I punish you with two days' barrack arrest. You are not serving in a French line regiment, but in the Foreign Legion. You understand, do you not, that in the Foreign Legion no man is taxed with his nationality. And in every respect it is very unwise to vex your corporal. *Ça y est.*'

At that the *légionnaire* laughed and quiet reigned once more.

My God, the heat was terrible. Then all at once a slashing, metallic sound. One of the Spaniards had pulled down the long bayonet that always hangs over a *légionnaire*'s bed, and was in the act of assaulting his countryman and comrade. The corporal sprang between the two and sent one flying to the right, the other to the left. In a second the whole place was in an uproar. The two Spaniards threw themselves upon each other, anxious to kill each other. The other *légionnaires* laughed and howled out through it all. . . .

At last the signal, '*Debout, légionnaires, debout!*' 'Up, up!' sounded down in the yard. The *siesta* was at an end.

This is what I wrote while lying half naked in my bed, groaning at the heat. The description has the advantage of the impressions of the moment. This was what happened when the *cafard* was at its "best."

Then again whole numbers of soldiers are affected by it in the same way. The *légionnaires* of half a company would put their heads together, planning some act of desperation. One time it would be mu-

---

1. *Monsieur le Caporal* was Corporal Wassermann's nickname, because in the eyes of the *légionnaires* he was far too particular in his manners and language when giving orders.

tiny *en masse*, at another time desertion in a body. This madness is well known wherever a company of *légionnaires* is stationed. In some kind of form it is always present. It is the cause of the horrible tattooing, of drinking and brawling; it is the reason for that peculiar longing for continual change, that restlessness typical of the Foreign Legion.

The *légionnaires* are themselves not aware what influence the *cafard* has on them. When an old *légionnaire* says grumpily, "*J'ai le cafard*," he is just telling his neighbours to keep clear of him, that he has a bad fit of the blues, that it is advisable for his comrades to leave him alone. He has no idea that a hidden power, like unto madness, is making him act in such a manner, he only believes himself to be in a bad humour. But the bad humour rises and increases, often driving him to murder, more often to suicide. The *légionnaire* cannot foresee the effects of the *cafard*. The typical *cafard demoniacs*, the old grumpy fellows who do their duty like machines and at other times hardly speak at all, are instinctively feared, as if their comrades knew that at any moment the least trifle could lead to an outbreak of the dormant madness.

I have witnessed such an explosion (that is the proper term for it). We had a man in our company who had served for many years in the Legion. He was a Frenchman and had worn the Legion's uniform for more than ten years. He got out of our way whenever he could, and when his duties were over, slunk away into lonely corners of the barrack-yard. Every fifth day he left the barracks, on payday, to return reeling, evidently drunk, just before evening muster. He never was rowdy, but silent as usual, he threw himself upon his bed. Where he went to, where he bought his wine, with whom he drank it, nobody knew.

One payday, when the half of our company was on guard-duty, he for once came back too late.

The barrack-gates had long been closed; Smith and I were still sitting on the bench in front of the guard-room, the sergeant and the other *légionnaires* were lying inside on their bunks. All at once the sentry at the gate called the officer on duty with the laconic report:

"*Sergeant—la porte!*"

The gate! Swearing, the man came with his keys. Outside stood the grumpy old *légionnaire*, swaying from side to side and his *kepi* at the back of his head.

"Bertillon?" the sergeant said, unlocking the gate. "You—old pig, you ought to know by this time when to come home."

Bertillon staggered in and remained standing in front of the sergeant.

"Be off with you and get into your quarters!" he commanded. "You can be jolly glad that your own company is on guard duty, else you would have been locked up at once. *Allez—schieb' los!*"

The old *légionnaire* stared at the sergeant. Suddenly, without saying a word, he hit him right in the face with his fist.

"*Aux armes!*" the reeling sergeant yelled. Bertillon had pulled out his bayonet and was slashing and hitting at every one, roaring like a wild beast. A terrible tussle ensued. We were twelve to one, but it took us more than a quarter of an hour to get the upper hand of the *cafard* madman, and every one had been more or less wounded by his bayonet. At length we contrived to throw blankets over his head, and strapping him up like a parcel, we threw him into the prison.

On opening the cell the next morning he was found dead. At the post-mortem examination the army surgeon stated that the bursting of an artery in the brain had been the cause of death.

These are the worst cases of *cafard*.

Generally the peculiar malady of the Foreign Legion shows itself in all kinds of peculiar whims. Smith's comical reciting of the *Koran* chapters was such a whim. Many developed some kind of fixed idea.

The cook of my company was an old *légionnaire* who had served in the Legion for fifteen years and was soon to be pensioned off; his fixed idea was that he was Bismarck's double. His name was Schlesinger. Like the German Prime Minister, he had the stature of a giant, and in his heavy face with the bald head, in the sharp eyes, there certainly was a slight resemblance to the features of the "man of iron." The Legion, being good-natured and having a great sense of humour, did old Schlesinger the favour of never calling him anything else but "Bismarck."

Herr von Rader was the first one to draw my attention to him. He had heard of the cook's peculiarity and . . . forthwith rushed to the kitchen. He lounged about the door till the cook, getting suspicious, came to see if the intruder intended stealing. Hardly had von Rader seen him, when he called out in astonishment: "Good gracious! that surely must be Bismarck!"

The cook drew himself up majestically and smiled condescendingly.

"Such a likeness!" in a surprised voice from von Rader.

"Very like—*n'est-ce pas?*" said Schlesinger, highly flattered.

"Really wonderful! You surely must be a relation of the Bismarck family? "

"That may be," nodded the cook, very much pleased. This was quite a new idea. It had never entered his head that he might be related to Bismarck.

"You're certainly a relation," said von Rader in a tone of conviction, "an illegitimate."

"*Très possible—très possible,*" the cook murmured, proud and happy. "Are you a young soldier?" he asked the man who had put the wonderful idea into his poor old *légionnaire's* head.

"That's so," groaned von Rader. "I am like you, and have once been something better. My father "(von Rader lowered his voice to a whisper as if he were disclosing the greatest secret), "my father was a count!"

Bismarck was much impressed by his announcement.

"And now I must starve in the Legion," added von Rader sadly.

"*Pas ça,*" said Schlesinger, and, disappearing into the kitchen, he returned with a large piece of roast pork. "*Tiens, camarade.* Tomorrow we will talk again about—about our ancestors. *Mais*—say nothing."

"Nothing," assured von Rader, putting his finger to his lips.

From that day the pseudo-Bismarck and the pseudo-count were seen together almost daily, and von Rader always had a piece of meat in his knapsack, when we had to eat dry bread in the drill pause.

If any one called the cook "Schlesinger" he was deeply offended and did not answer; even the officers called him Bismarck.

There was another *légionnaire* I cannot forget—Little Krügerle. His whim was—to steal grapes. A very funny idea, for Krügerle never ate grapes himself; he did not like them. With great trouble he got them into the barracks and then gave them away.

His one idea was to steal the grapes.

This was his *cafard,* his special rage against the possessors of vineyards. But his *cafard* had its own tale. . . .

Grapes were worth very little in Algeria, but when every year at the grape harvest three thousand *légionnaires* strolled in the evenings along the paths beside the vineyards, when each *légionnaire* ate about five pounds of grapes, taking another ten pounds under his cloak—then the Spanish grape-farmers grew angry. They sent a deputation to the colonel, declaring that his *légionnaires* were worse than a locust-plague. The colonel abused them all and sent out a command that all who transgressed again would be punished. The *légionnaires* laughed—were a little more careful, but stole quite as many grapes as formerly. Seeing that it would not do like this, the Spaniards engaged Arabs, gave them small-shot guns and told them not to spare the offenders. The following morning the army surgeon was much astonished, on going his daily round, to find sixty-five *légionnaires* wounded by small shot.

The extraction of all the small shot took so much time that he got furious and went to the colonel and complained. The latter, having an idea what was the matter, examined the "invalids," who promptly told a great story of having been suddenly attacked by Arabs. The colonel laughed and ordered them all to be locked up for four weeks on bread and water.

Now the Spaniards were left in peace, because the grapes were not worth while being shot and locked up for, the *légionnaires* said sadly.

But from this time dated little Krügerle's *cafard*. Every day he went out to steal grapes. With the greatest patience and cunning he crawled about in the vineyards and stole grapes. Once he was shot and ran right back to the barracks and into the soldiers' room. Five minutes later, all the fifteen men there were busily occupied in digging the countless shot out of their comrade's back—with pocket-knives! .

Krügerle underwent the operation with more or less tranquillity—but it was worth suffering a little; if he had gone to the surgeon, four weeks of *cellule* arrest would have been his lot.

He swore great oaths—but went stealing grapes again the following day.

The germ of madness, of tragedy, always lies hidden in the *cafard*. I was a witness of the following tragedy.

In our room in the corner by the window an Austrian had his bed. His name was Bauer. He had joined the company with a new batch of recruits, shortly after I did, in good health, fresh and curious like all the other recruits: an average man, who did not easily learn the French words of command, but did his work conscientiously. Week by week he got quieter. Stupidly he did his work and spoke to nobody. In his free time he sat on his bed moodily staring in front of him. Now and then he would be punished for neglecting his uniform, but this did not seem to make any impression on him at all. He returned from prison as moody as before. Nobody took any notice of him. All at once the poor quiet creature became the centre of attraction, an object of ridicule and enmity, and for weeks the gossip of the Legion's quarters.

Suddenly Bauer was attacked by a most ravenous appetite. If possible he was quieter than formerly; but when the midday soup appeared, he fell over it like a wild animal, devouring it greedily, and greedily he watched us while we were eating. When we had finished, he crept up to the table, examining the empty dishes in the hope of finding a few drops left. After this he would rush down to the kitchen to the old cook to beg some leavings from him. The other men in the room were so brutalised by their own misfortunes in life that they only looked upon this poor devil as a clown to serve for their amusement.

They threw pieces of bread into corners, and yelled with pleasure when Bauer crawled about on all-fours under the beds to look for the coveted morsel. They poured petroleum into his soup, and were wild with delight when the poor fellow nevertheless emptied the dish greedily.

Day by day Bauer grew worse. From the other soldiers' quarters, even from the other companies, the *légionnaires* came at soup-time to our room to inspect the prodigy. All the time he sat crouching on his bed, smiling vacantly and gobbling down whatever he could get. He would gnaw at the dry bone held out to him by a *légionnaire* with the same grin as he would chew a piece of hard leather given to him by another man. It was the beginning of insanity. . . .

Soon the whole regiment was talking about the man with the un-appeasable appetite. If anyone wished to have a joke, they brought the glutton a dry crust or a piece of hard Legion biscuit, just to watch him devour it. For weeks these scenes occurred, without the authorities thinking it necessary to interfere.

The end came suddenly. One day we only found half-chewed crusts on our table instead of the usual daily portion of bread. Bauer had stolen away from his work and eaten our rations!

The *légionnaires* threw themselves upon him—where their own comforts were concerned it was no joking matter. One of them struck the poor devil, who, biting and scratching and hitting at every one, shrieked like a madman. The watch was roused, and the poor fellow, chained hand and foot, was carried across to the infirmary.

Three days after, the eleventh company conducted a small black cart to the graveyard of Sidi-bel-Abbès. In the rudely made coffin on the cart lay the remains of *Légionnaire* Bauer. In the infirmary he had smashed his head against the wall. . . . At the grave the captain said briefly, in a cold voice: "*Recevez les derniers adieux de votre chef et de vos camarades.*"

This was his funeral sermon.

CHAPTER 11

The Deserters

Even Herr von Rader had the *cafard*—the fever to desert—and his good humour diminished perceptibly under its influence. In low cunning the equal of the oldest and craftiest *légionnaire*, he had quite got the trick of decorating himself, and certainly got along much better than most of the other recruits. But, as a veteran on the high road of life, he had a very highly developed sense of the practical side of human affairs. To take and not to give had always been his most sacred rule of life; living without working was for him the acme of human cleverness. Now, however, Herr von Rader began to reckon out for himself, with a face that got longer and longer, the Legion's pet arithmetic example: that he had to do an immense amount of work and got little or no pay for it.

He found this very trying.

"My friend," he said to me once, "I'm off. I just guess I won't bother you with details, but I'm sorry to have to tell you that this honourable regiment will have to get on as best it can without me. I'm going to clear out."

I warned him and kept telling him that it was utter folly to desert in this happy-go-lucky way without civilian's clothes and without any money.

Herr von Rader merely shook his head:

It's true enough that I've a large balance of poverty! On the other hand, I've a thundering lot of impudence—an absolutely immense and overwhelming quantity of impudence—and I guess, in spite of everything, I'll take that little pleasure trip and have a look at the neighbourhood. Somewhere round here there must be a nigger tribe who would consider it an honour when a chap like me with a real white skin does some swell conjuring for them. Why, they'll jump at the chance of making me their medicine man. Anyway, I'm off! If you're a wise man, you'll come too. It'll be fine enough even if it does not last for long. And I'll tell you a secret: in the sergeants' room the big service revolver is hanging comfortably on the wall. I've a sort of an idea that that piece of property will be off about the same time as me—on French leave! That's a great consolation for me, quite apart from the fact that I shall be damned glad to annoy that fool of a sergeant! Won't you come?

I declined with thanks.

Herr von Rader now sought other followers. In every spare moment he gathered a following from among the young men around his bed. They lounged about and smoked cigarettes forging their plans for flight. More than once I went and listened to them and more than once I gave them a warning, but they were so wrapped up in their idea that all good advice was quite wasted. They wanted to make a bee-line for the south, marching only at night and avoiding all houses and villages. Then they thought of going west and working through into Morocco.

One of them had found an old map of Northern Africa, and on this they had marked out their route. Their bayonets and the revolver they were going to steal were to be their weapons. They were not in the least afraid of Arabs or Moroccans, and about provisions they didn't worry themselves very much, as Herr von Rader cold-bloodedly pointed out that they were six strong men and could easily procure the necessaries of life by force. In reality they were very indifferent as to all these details. The only idea that they had in their heads was that they would soon have done with their wretched lives as *légionnaires*, and roam at large, free men once more.

They were thoroughly infected with the fever for desertion, which was ever to be found in the Legion. Plans for flight and their feasibility were ever being discussed in whispers, and this formed a part of the Legion's atmosphere—desertion was always the favourite topic of conversation in quarters and in the canteen. This was only natural. There is not a single man in the Legion who does not sooner or later repent his folly, recognising that it was the maddest thing he ever did in his life when he signed that ominous contract in the enlistment bureau. He has to work as he never worked in his life before, and he has less money in his pocket than in the most needy times of his civil life.

Even if he had been a miserable beggar, a wretched copper had not such an enormous value in his eyes nor had it been so hard to earn as in these days of poverty in the Foreign Legion. He is wretchedly poor, living under the strictest military discipline, working hard and getting less than nothing out of his life. At first the strangeness of his surroundings has a certain charm: but the harder he has to work and the oftener he becomes acquainted with the heavy penalties which no *légionnaire* escapes for long, the quicker comes the lust for freedom.

The idea of flight gradually ripens in him. He talks about it with his friends; in every spare moment he washes and cleans for the non-commissioned officers to earn a few coppers, and every evening he sits with the veterans, with the old grey-haired fellows who have breathed the air of the Legion so long that they are no use for any other sort of work, and who, as if under a spell, no matter how often they have sworn never to don the red trousers again, always come back again to the Legion. They know Algeria like the palm of their own hand and gladly sell their priceless wisdom for a litre of canteen wine. But in this case good advice is not worth much.

Money is the main necessity for flight. If good intentions counted for anything in the matter, the percentage of deserters would reach a fabulous figure; but the poor fellows who go out on foot, without a penny in their pockets, very seldom get away and are generally brought back in a few days by the *gendarmes*. Hunger and thirst almost always drive them into the Arab villages or to the Spanish peasant settlements on the main roads, which are so often patrolled that detection is unavoidable. Then is the wisdom of the old *légionnaire* a vain thing indeed—against enemies like hunger and thirst the truant can do nothing.

In addition to the lust for freedom the *légionnaire* has generally got the *cafard*: a feeling of hatred for anything connected with the Legion, the extraordinary impulse which leads him to undertake the maddest and most hopeless things rather than stay a day longer in the Legion. When they are as ill as this the poor fellows run off no matter where, without the slightest consideration or preparation.

The Legion has coined a special expression for this kind of desertion: "Going on pump"—in French, "*Aller au poump*." An extraordinary word of unknown origin.

You "go on pump." One evening as we sat in quarters cleaning our leather equipment, an old *légionnaire*, an Austrian, suddenly got up.

"You damned set of fools," he cried, "I'm going out. I'm going on pump."

As he spoke he buckled on his bayonet.

"I hope I'll never see the blasted lot of you again."

He went out and never returned.

Several weeks afterwards there was shown to us at roll-call the photograph of a body that had been horribly maimed. It was the Austrian. A patrol had found him by the Morocco frontier. The officer in command, to whose equipment according to regulation a camera belonged, had taken the photograph. Each company in the Legion got a copy of this awful picture, in order to identify the corpse. The regiment has quite a series of these pictures, all showing a man's naked body, hacked about in the most appalling fashion. This is the work of the Moroccan brigands, to whom the *légionnaire*, staggering hither and thither under the influence of the *cafard*, is a real source of joy. His uniform and bayonet are priceless possessions, easily won with a few sword-strokes. Besides, there is the consideration that Allah and his prophet reward a pious deed like torturing a dog of a Christian.

Hundreds of *légionnaires* who have started out in *cafard* have met with this awful death in the desert, martyred, maimed and tortured.

In general, however, the *légionnaire* finds going on pump, this flight into the desert, this mad rush for freedom without any real goal and without any sort of preparation, something quite natural that everybody tries once at any rate in the course of his career. In *cafard*. . . .

As a rule the men desert in little groups, without any equipment but the uniform they wear and the bayonet that clanks at their side. They go forth at night, before nine o'clock, while the barrack gates are still open, and run, under cover of the darkness, madly through the sandy vineyards. They are miserably cold in the chilly African night, and the pangs of hunger soon assail them. But they keep going on: they are accustomed to accomplish miracles of marching even when loaded with the Legion's heavy baggage; without it they cover enormous distances.

Five minutes at the double with that long cat-like stride of the Legion which never tires those who have once got the knack of it—and then five minutes' marching. They go on like this without stopping all through the night, and in the morning the truants are a good sixty *kilometres* from the garrison. Arriving at some lonely farm or other in the grey of the morning, they obtain a crust of bread and a sip of wine. It is very seldom the sympathetic heart of the Spaniard that takes pity on them: no, it is more often the bayonets which advise him to be obliging and conciliatory. In the daytime the *poumpistes* hide among the rocks or bury themselves in a deep hole in the sand.

When night comes on they start on their way once more, ever southwards, keeping their bearings by the stars as they have learnt to do in the Legion—for a very different purpose it is true. When they hear the sound of horses' hoofs they take cover in deadly terror and lie for hours, still as mice, until the patrol has long passed out of sight below the horizon. Thus the days pass by. Bands of energetic and enterprising runaways often terrorise the Arabs in the lonely settlements for weeks on end, until the oppressed ones send for help and a fight results in which the deserters are of course sadly worsted.

Desperate fellows "on pump," who are determined to reach Morocco at any price, sometimes succeed in getting hold of a rifle. They have then a weapon to defend themselves against the brigands. They cannot take their own rifles with them, for with rifles they would never be allowed to pass the barrack gates.

A tough old veteran, who knows the frontier, marches with the utmost care. He knows that there is a triple row of tents, a quarter of a *kilometre* apart. One dark night he creeps through. This operation takes a long time to carry out. The tents, it is true, are a long way apart from each other, and it seems easy enough to get through. But this is only at first sight. For every 200 yards there stands a sentry guarding the line till the next tent is reached.

The line of tents is almost endless. Were the deserter to attempt to creep through direct or even in a slanting direction, he could not possibly avoid being noticed by one of the sentries who are stationed in a triangular arrangement. But he knows the trick. He creeps through 100 yards from a sentry and then strikes off at an angle of 45 degrees until he reaches the next row. Then straight on once more and then off again at an angle. . . .

Now he works himself, crawling on his stomach and burying himself in the sand for hours at a time, up to a tent in the outside line. He steps silently into the tent, feels about with care—and he is the possessor of a rifle and a cartridge-belt. Thus armed he has now a chance of life and of getting safely across Morocco.

In most cases, however, after a few days of golden freedom, a freedom consisting of perpetual marching and ceaseless hunger, the man on pump meets his fate in the shape of a band of mounted *Goums*,[1]

1. *Goums* is the Legion's name for the Arab *gendarmes*.

and finds himself, after a very short space of time, looking down the muzzles of their revolvers. He then has to go back the same way he came, fastened by a long chain to one of the *Goums'* horses, panting and coughing with the exertion of keeping up with the horse, which he must do if he doesn't want to be dragged over the sand and stones. Thus he is taken from station to station till the garrison is reached. If he is lucky enough not to have lost any part of his equipment and has not been absent more than a week, he is tried by the regiment, and gets off with sixty days' *cellule*—solitary confinement in the dark. If, however, any part of his uniform is missing, he is tried for theft and desertion by the court-martial in Oran, which is noted for its Draconic sentences.

Traveaux forcés, penal servitude for years, is then his fate—a penalty which usually means death, for there are very few constitutions that can stand the terrible life in the penal settlements.

Rader and his friends were *poumpistes* of this type. One evening the man of strong language and never-failing wit was missing when the roll was called. Several others were reported missing from various rooms, and the next morning the whole company knew that six Germans had deserted *en bloc*.

The sergeant of our section made a list of the uniform and equipment Herr von Rader had left behind. He cursed, as only a lazy sergeant in the Legion can curse, his own personal bad luck because the six deserters, being in his company, now gave him a lot of work and worry. At the evening roll-call the colour-sergeant appeared in person in our room and ordered Corporal Wassermann to take good care that no more of the men under his charge deserted: otherwise he'd make it d—— d hot for him. The captain, however, sent for all the Germans in his company.

He made us a long speech in the company's *bureau*:

We had all served our time in Germany and we ought really to be content with the life in his company. There was no flogging in the Legion! When anybody thought he had a ground for complaint he should report himself at once to the captain. The Legion was a regiment of foreigners, and one nation was treated in exactly the same way as another: a German soldier in it had naturally exactly the same rights as everyone else. He would be very sorry if his men took to deserting. It was quite hopeless to try! A description of the deserters had been telegraphed long ago to all the stations in Algeria, the police all along the coast were on the lookout, and in a few days we should see the truants brought back to the regiment.

"You only get into trouble when you desert, as it is very heavily punished!"

"The whole thing is this," said Smith when we came back into our room. "The cap'n is champion fencer of France, and thinks he must be always practising in the fencing saloon! He hasn't the least idea what things really look like in the company!"

Even a raw recruit knew much more of what went on in the company than its leader. The non-commissioned officers took very good care that the captain did not learn too much. . . .

In reality the colour-sergeant and the non-commissioned officers were all-powerful. The captain was merely what one might call the owner of the business, who signed the punishment sheets and reports which his managers laid before him, without bothering his head about details. The non-coms had the mess-allowance in their hands, put down whatever men they pleased on the punishment sheet for absolutely nothing at all, and would very quickly have done to death anyone who made a complaint, even if at first he got his rights by complaining.

"By the beard of the Prophet," laughed Smith, "I'd like to see what happened to the chap who made a complaint. Why, the whole bally lot of non-coms would be down on him in less than no time, and in a couple of weeks he'd be a *Zephyr* in the penal battalion. That's what happens when you complain, *Signor Capitano*. But he's quite right about deserting is our champion captain. We do see most of 'em again."

Then he went over to Rassedin and asked him if he thought that Rader and the other five *poumpistes* would get away. Rassedin shook his head and laughed, making with his thumb and forefinger that counting gesture which means paying all the world over.

"No money," he said dryly.

The other veterans too thought that Rader and the other five were not the sort of men who would succeed in surmounting the difficulties of a flight unprovided with money.

The flight of the six comrades was an inexhaustible topic of conversation in the company. Smith used to spin one yarn after another of mad bids for freedom. Two of these histories I shall never forget.

While Smith was in the second battalion at Saida, there were two brothers in his company, two Englishmen of good birth. The final and maddest freak of their mad lives landed them in the Legion. When

131

their family learnt that they were wearing the Legion's uniform, they did all they could to procure their freedom. In vain! Petitions to the French Secretary of War were of no avail, and the English Consul in Algiers naturally refused to intervene. Finally the two brothers were sent a large sum of money and they tried their luck at deserting. They were no farther than Saida station when they were arrested and marched back to prison.

As soon as they were free again they made a second attempt at flight and got as far as Oran. But their descriptions had been telegraphed there and they were arrested as they were going on board the steamer. This time they were sent for six months to the penal battalion.

The poor devils must have written despairing letters home. Their relations were determined to get them free at any price. With an English merchant as go-between, they bribed a Levantine, who hired an automobile and waited days and days by Saida, in the neighbourhood where the convicts had to work. After long delay the brothers succeeded in escaping at night from their tent. They reached the appointed rendezvous in safety, found the Levantine with his motor waiting for them, and started off as quickly as the sand would allow.

The automobile, however, had attracted notice in Saida, and the military authorities came at once on the idea that these dauntless deserters had hit on the unusual method of flight by motorcar. Telegrams flew from station to station, and the Arab police barricaded a narrow part of the road a little north of Sidi-bel-Abbès, which passes at this point through a rocky part of the country, absolutely impassable for vehicles.

A short time afterwards the motor came up. The runaways took no notice of the warnings of the *gendarmes* who rode to meet them, and crashed at full speed into the pile of stones. The motor was overturned, the two deserters being killed immediately. The Levantine was seriously injured and brought into the hospital at Sidi-bel-Abbès, where he died a few days later.

The other story is a really sad one.

An Austrian engineer had, as a young man, for some reason or other enlisted in the Foreign Legion. After a while he managed to escape and worked his way home to Austria again. He must have been a clever fellow, for he soon gained a distinguished position in his profession. Fortune smiled upon him. He made a notable invention, which made him a wealthy man. Ambition led him to send the machine he had invented to the World's Exhibition in Paris. In the distinguished engineer nobody would recognise the deserter from the Foreign Legion—at least so he thought. But cruel fate willed otherwise. Standing by his machine at the exhibition he was recognised by an officer from his company who was just then on leave in Paris.

The officer did his duty as a soldier and had the deserter arrested. At one blow the man who had worked his way from the depths of poverty to the top of his profession, who looked upon the days in the Legion as merely a dark shadow on his life, became once more a *légionnaire*. A few days in a Parisian military prison, a few hours' journey by rail in a prisoners' compartment, the short sea-voyage to Oran, the cruel minutes before the court-martial—and then perpetual, blunting work in an Algerian mine, truly a living death. And thus this man had to live for many a long month, till the horrible climate carried him off. . . . .

Flight from the Legion is always a risky and difficult undertaking, risky since there is always the severest punishment waiting for the deserter who gets caught. Even the possession of really plentiful means is no guarantee for a successful flight. There are so many hindrances to surmount, such a mountain of difficulties to be climbed.

To begin at the beginning.

The Ghetto of Sidi-bel-Abbès supplies the clothes. Buying civilian clothes is the first chapter of a *légionnaire's* flight, the first part of his preparations for which the would-be deserter needs not only money but also a finely developed talent for haggling and bargaining. To open negotiations is very easy: the *légionnaire* simply addresses a passer-by in one of the little alleys and whispers to him that he knows of someone who would perhaps buy civilian clothes. In one case in a hundred the passer-by shakes his head and goes his way. In the ninety-nine other cases he looks pleased, and in just such a whisper tells the *légionnaire* to follow him into his house without attracting attention. Once there, the bargaining begins. Heaps of old clothes are fetched, until something is found somewhere about the customer's size. Boots, shirt, collar, hat, and tie are all found. To an honest man of business the transaction would seem somewhat strange.

These Ghetto transactions have an underlying principle of their own: furnish as poor goods as possible at as high a price as you can get! The buyer is already nervous at the prospect of his flight, so, in spite of all, he pays an absolutely fabulous price. Fifty *francs* is usually the price of an old suit, of which the trousers come, perhaps, from Germany, the waistcoat from France, and the coat from Italy, and which would be very dear at ten *francs*. The "business friend" next claims a gold piece for allowing the *légionnaire* to change his clothes in his house; a further gold piece arranges for the care of his uniform, which a *légionnaire* who is at all careful will not be persuaded so easily to leave in the lurch. For the deserter captured without his uniform is tried for theft by court-martial, and the military tribunal in Oran always passes sentence of a long term of penal servitude.

But the man of Israel is willing enough—provided he gets a gold piece for it—to take care that the uniform and entire equipment of his customer is safely preserved for the poor regiment. Neatly bound together the uniform lies idle for a few days. Then, one dark night, a youth from the Ghetto throws the parcel over the wall of the barracks. A ticket has been pinned on beforehand, on which the name and number of the owner has been written so that the gentlemen in the quartermaster's office needn't cudgel their brains wondering how to register this parcel from heaven.

All so considerate!

The runaway, however, wanders through the alleys of the Jewish quarter and the streets of Sidi-bel-Abbès, taking great care to avoid instinctively saluting the officers and non-coms he meets. His money, with which he bought his civilian clothes, and of which there is still enough for his railway journey and passage, is a mighty help to him.

He must not attract notice anywhere; he must bridle his tongue, lest the curious French which is individual to the Legion betray him, and he must act the role of the harmless traveller to a nicety. He naturally cannot begin his journey from the station of Sidi-bel-Abbès, which is watched by a commando of the Legion's non-commissioned officers day and night. No, he must go on foot to one of the stations on the way to his destination; the farther from Sidi-bel-Abbès he is, the less likely he is to attract attention. So he makes a long night march, keeping a sharp look-out for the patrols of Arab police. Then comes the railway journey to a coast town. The only two towns that come in question are Oran and the town of Algiers, since regular lines of steamers only run from these two ports.

Oran is mostly avoided, because it is so near to Sidi-bel-Abbès, and because there are so many of the Legion's officers to be met with there. The journey to Algiers, on the other hand, is very expensive, and it often happens that the truant's money is exhausted, and he lands there penniless. In this case German *légionnaires* usually go to the German Consulate, but only receive the stereotyped reply that there is no money at the Consul's disposal "for purposes like this."

The Consulate is not only powerless to help them, but, into the bargain, is one of the best and most efficient mouse-traps a French *gendarme* could want. Old *légionnaires* always give you the same warning: "For the Lord's sake don't go to the Consul in Algiers." If, in spite of this, a deserter does go to the Consul, he is merely told that he cannot possibly gain assistance there.

And now the trap begins to do its work. The police in Algiers know well enough that there are a great many escaped *légionnaires* among the men who come to the Consulate. When any one comes out looking in the least bit suspicious, they receive him tenderly and inquire lovingly about his papers. The deserter is then done for. . . .

I should like to know whether the German Consul in Algiers has the slightest idea that, in all innocence, he has been the ruin of so many German *légionnaires*.

The runaway whose money has been swallowed up by the railway journey and who cannot pay his passage over sea, must in most cases give himself up for lost. It is generally only a question of a few days till he is arrested. A careless word in a wine-shop, a lame excuse when he seeks work and can show no papers—in short, the whole system of denunciation which is so flourishing in Algiers very soon hands him over to the police.

And even when he has money enough to pay his passage on one of the Mediterranean lines, and has his ticket safe in his pocket, he is not yet in safety. Most of the runaways who have succeeded in reaching Algiers make the mistake of taking a passage on one of the German or English lines of steamers, and is arrested at the eleventh hour as he goes on board. It is on the foreign ships that they keep a specially sharp eye. On the French boats, on the other hand, which ply between Algiers and Oran, you don't need any papers or even a passport, because the authorities look upon these boats as an internal French means of communication.

The route from Algiers to Tunis is absolutely safe for the deserter. There, nobody notices him in the enormous rush of the Levantine traffic, and he needs no passport to cross to an Italian port. But the expense is enormous.

Among the *légionnaires* who desert, the number of those who can escape in civilian clothes by the comparatively safe way of the railway and the Mediterranean boats is very small. Travelling costs money. . . . A flight over the town of Algiers needs really quite a little capital—150 *francs* at least. This is a very low estimate, for the purchase of clothes alone takes about seventy *francs*. How few of the men in the Legion can raise such a sum like this!

In most cases they are poor devils who have no one in the wide world who could or would send them a sum of this sort; most of them never had a *franc* to their name while they were in the Legion, to say nothing of a gold coin. Men like this are seldom successful in their flight, even when they spend months and months in preparation and discuss their route a hundred times over with the veterans of the Legion. They don't run blindly into the desert like the *poumpistes*, who don't really want more than a few days of runaway freedom. Their way is also to the coast. In uniform! On foot!

In these two expressions there is expressed the deserter's whole difficulty. Although the distance from Sidi-bel-Abbès to the coast is only about one hundred *kilometres*, not a very great stretch for a *légion-naire* who is accustomed to long marches? it is beset with danger for every yard of the way. The runaway can be recognised a long way off by his uniform. True, he only marches by night. But the starlit nights of Algeria are very bright, and he has to creep from rock to rock and from hollow to hollow, to avoid being seen by the patrols. By day he lies motionless in the sand. He suffers hunger and thirst for days on end, and lives on fruits, which he steals when hunger drives him to risk discovery.

When he has reached the coast in safety, the game of hide-and-seek begins anew. He often lies for days in some little coast town, where the Mediterranean tramp-steamers touch, concealed in a shed or in some old boat on the shore, till a ship carrying the German or English flag comes into port. He swims out to this ship in the middle of the night, climbs on board, and hides in one of the ship's boats, or in the coal-bunker. He first makes his appearance when the ship is on the high seas as a more or less pleasant surprise for the captain. He is now safe—they can hardly throw him overboard. There are, moreover, a great many captains who shut their eyes when a runaway of this sort is discovered, and even if the ship is still lying in port do not give him up. There are some even who carry their humanity so far as to stand a certain amount of unpleasantness with the authorities for his sake.

These are mostly German ships, and above all, ships from Hamburg. Deserters from the Legion land over and over again in the old Hansa town, and again and again you may read in the Hamburg daily papers that deserters have arrived with such and such a ship, and have been taken charge of by the police authorities. Now and then they go just as they stand, in their uniform, with bayonet and all the rest of it, to the paper's offices and tell the worried editor about their life and sorrows in the Legion. . . .

These are those who have had luck; the tiny proportion of penniless deserters who are successful in their flight. Not freedom but prison awaits the large majority at the finish of their attempt. The Arab *gendarmes* are paid a bonus on the deserters they arrest, which amounts to many thousand *francs* a year!

The regiment is acquainted with many other means of desertion, if by "desertion" you understand every means by which the deserter can free himself from work in the Legion. In the terrible heat of summer, when the difference in temperature between day and night is simply enormous, sickness, in many a grim form, stalks through Algeria. The drinking water becomes infected, and typhoid sets in: the *légionnaire* who is tired of active service can be pretty sure of a long spell of illness.

But to make quite certain he helps matters artificially—with an extraordinary measure in vogue in the Legion: he drinks a mixture of *absinthe* and milk. Every veteran in the Legion swears this hellish drink never fails to bring on an attack of fever! The object of this suicidal method of desertion is naturally to avoid work in the Legion by a long spell of sickness—its object is always attained; mostly so effectively that the man never takes his place on parade again, but rests for ever in the Legion's cemetery!

In the same way self-mutilation may be met with: the chopping off of a finger which renders the *légionnaire* unfit for active service. Others simulate illness or madness. This the suspiciousness and brutality of the doctors in the Legion renders very difficult. Now and then a *légionnaire* with a will of iron manages to play the comedy of madness successfully.

The means employed are sometimes rather drastic. Some years before I entered the Legion, a Belgian served in my company who shammed for a whole year. He dirtied the men's quarters in such a fashion that his comrades fell upon him and ill-treated him in every possible way, but he merely answered their curses and reprisals with an inane laugh. Neither curses nor blows seemed to make the least difference to him.

This fellow had grit. He played his part as a lunatic, as unpleasant for himself as well as for others, without ever wavering. They shut him up, they compelled him to do the hardest work, they brought him into hospital and well-nigh starved him or tortured him with drugs; he was confined for weeks in the dark, he was sent to the hospital at Daya and treated with cold water—all in vain! His method and his smile remained unchanged! After thirteen months the doctors felt themselves checkmated, gave up the job as hopeless and certified him mad. The colonel, purely out of curiosity, sent for the lunatic, who must needs have an attack of his particular malady in the regimental *bureau* itself.

As soon, however, as he was home again in Belgium, he wrote postcards to the officers and to several members of his company.... He had foiled them all and they were the idiots! The most unmitigated ass of them in his humble opinion was the regimental doctor! If possible the surgeon-major in the Algerian corps was a bigger fool still!

Tremendous energy is, however, necessary to bring a sham of this sort to a successful issue, and cases like this constitute a tiny minority. The doctors in the Foreign Legion are both clever and suspicious and the result is that there is always a good dose of Legion's brutality included in their treatment. All those who reported themselves sick, and hadn't some outward and visible sign of their ailment to show, were treated from beginning to end as shams.

Our *médecin*-major was an especial terror to the *légionnaires*. I only came into personal contact with him twice; the first time was on a manoeuvre march when he refused me the medicine I wanted, and the other time was when I was vaccinated. There was an epidemic of smallpox in Sidi-bel-Abbès, and the whole of the Legion had to be vaccinated as quickly as possible. We were marched by companies into the great drill-hall where *Monsieur le Major* and his assistants were at work.

Such a method of vaccination as this man employed I have never seen in my life and I have been vaccinated at least a dozen times. I am acquainted with every method of vaccination, from the gentle lancet-prick employed in Germany to the method in use in America, where they pare away the skin with a piece of ivory. As our company marched past the assembled doctors in Indian file I saw to my astonishment that the men were bleeding severely. When my turn came I flinched involuntarily—the doctor drove the lancet three times so forcibly into my upper arm that a regular fountain of blood spurted out.

It was pure brutality. Nothing more or less. This was typical of the man. It was his custom, the first time a man reported himself ill, to send him back to his company and give him three days' arrest for shamming. If the fellow appeared again he tried the effect of emetics followed by a long period of starvation. The only time he was supposed to be reasonable was when he saw symptoms of typhoid, which was his special hobby.

The Legion was thoroughly afraid of the hospital! They were desperate fellows indeed who tried shamming!

The topic of desertion from the Foreign Legion is well-nigh inexhaustible. When the transports sail from Oran or Marseilles to Indo-China with relief companies of the Legion on board, the Suez Canal is a favourite means of deserting. According to the Canal regulations the steamers must slacken speed in the narrow straits of Suez, and the *légionnaire* takes the opportunity to jump overboard. He swims the short stretch to land and is then safe. The sentries on the transports may not use firearms in the international waters of the Suez Canal, and therefore cannot fire on the deserter as he swims. Neither is extradition from the English or Egyptian authorities to be feared.

Several of these transports from the Foreign Legion pass through the Suez Canal every year, and these desertions are so frequent that the Ghetto of Port Said pays a fixed price of ten shillings for the capital service boots of the Legion!

Desertions *en masse* occur now and then, but these may be classed as mutinies rather than as desertions. In Southern Algeria, in the loneliness of the desert, the garrison of some small fort occasionally breaks out, marching for the Morocco frontier. The next bevy of troops soon brings the runaways back again, and even if it comes to a shot or two the superiority of the numbers against them soon brings the mutineers to reason. A mutiny like this generally ends in the mutineers being shot. An act of this sort is nothing else than an outbreak of madness caused by the dreadful monotony of service on the lonely stations in the desert. It is an outbreak of the *cafard*! The poor devils should be treated by a doctor instead of being sentenced by a court-martial.

The Foreign Legion is a fruitful field for hypnotic suggestion. In my time a number of *légionnaires* deserted from Sidi-bel-Abbès, with the intention of fighting their way through to Morocco. Morocco was just then talked about till the idea became surrounded with a sort of halo. The attempt itself was pretty hopeless the men were driven to it by the suggestive power of the words, *"le Maroc."*

Morocco was the Legion's fairyland, the land the soldier longed for. Not a single day went by without a rumour of fighting in Morocco raising excitement in the Foreign Legion to fever pitch. Dark war-clouds were gathering on the horizon. From the frontier there came continual reports of the intrigues of the pretender, and in the inland of Morocco mighty battles were fought at short intervals. Among the watchful officers of French Africa everyone was certain that the internal troubles in Morocco were not merely the petty splutterings of the usual native fireworks, but the first sparks of a mighty bonfire.

The Foreign Legion knew of this; then all that was discussed in the officers' mess filtered through to the regiment through its own various private channels.

Orderlies came rushing into the barracks in a fever of excitement as soon as they came off duty in the mess and told their friends in the Legion all about the heated debates that had taken place and which all revolved around Morocco. The servants of the staff officers brought news of Moroccan visitors closeted with their masters; *Spahis* who had served their time in the Morocco frontier garrisons and who were quartered on the regiment on their way through to Oran, told how sharp duty on the frontier now was, and how the garrisons were perpetually being strengthened.

The veterans put their heads together and discussed the prospects of a bloody war! They had wonderful stories to tell of the golden treasures of Morocco, of the jewels that the better classes wore, and in their fancy they pictured an Eldorado of plundered wealth and booty. These mysterious rumours grew from day to day. More than half of the regiment's officers were ordered to the little frontier towns, and it was not unnatural when the Legion found in this a sure sign of fighting to come.

With a broad smirk, an orderly brought the news that the colonel had engaged two masters to teach him Arabic, and it was easy to see how proud he was of the enormous supply of ammunition which was sent out from France. Recruiting began with zeal in the *Spahi* barracks opposite. Arab recruits with their splendid horses joined daily. Sections for telegraph duty went off to the frontier to see to the old wires and to lay new ones; volunteers were called for to form a corps for the heliographs, and veterans whose time was up got the tip from one or other of the officers that it would be very much to their advantage to stay on and not to take their dismissal just then. . . .

In this roundabout way, through non-coms, orderlies, and soldier servants, everything was perhaps very much distorted, but it all sounded very probable and typical. The Legion is like a mighty ear-trumpet—through its countless channels it gathers up the officers' gossip and intrigues for its own uses, and really knows a good deal about the state of affairs in Northern Africa; it knows that the military circles at the head of affairs in Algeria have their own axe to grind, and that the clever catch-phrase *"penetration pacifique"* was formed in an officers' club, and that greedy squinting at Morocco is as old as the occupation of Algeria!

It was as if everyone stood under the ban of a mesmerist. The longing for *le Maroc* spread to the *légionnaires*, who gave practical evidence of their longing for change and excitement, deserting in crowds. Most of them met their deaths. The border tribes cut their throats.

Others had more luck. In the army of the pretender, the present Sultan, Mulai Hafid, there used to be several officers who were once soldiers of the Foreign Legion!

CHAPTER 12

A Chapter on Punishments

"*Nom de Dieu!—voila les poumpistes!*" cried the sergeant of the guard at the barrack gates. Every one sprang up. We of the guard (my company was on guard that day) crowded round the gate; the adjutant *vaguemestre*, the regimental postmaster, ran out of his little office opposite the guard-room; a couple of officers came up, and *légionnaires* streamed out from everywhere in a wild rush for the entrance to the barracks.

"The *poumpistes* have come back!" they cried to each other.

It was in fact the truants from our company, poor Rader and his five friends. They were indeed a pitiful sight. Two *gendarmes* brought them in. They were all six bound together by a thin steel chain. Their dirty uniforms hung around them in rags; they were faint and emaciated and looked dead tired. Their faces were scarred. Rader had a blood-stained bandage round his right arm. In their eyes you could read the deadly fear of the punishment that awaited them.

They had, of course, been treated pretty badly by the *gendarmes*. They looked round them shyly, ashamed of their helplessness and of their fetters. Herr von Rader alone had not lost his sense of humour.

"How are you? Glad to see you!" he said to the sergeant! "I am back again all right."

In the little *bureau* of the officer of the day the two *gendarmes* had their depositions taken and received the usual receipt from the regiment for the safe delivery of the deserters. They withdrew looking very pleased with themselves, for this receipt was worth 25 *francs*, entitling them to their reward.

The *poumpistes* were kept waiting in front of the guard-room, still joined together by the chain. When Herr von Rader noticed me, he greeted me with many head-shakings:

"Damned rotten business!" he said quite loud. "*Mein Freund*, they didn't make me a medicine man after all. The conjuring didn't work! All at once five damned Arab *gendarmes* rode up to us, holding their revolvers under our noses. I couldn't conjure them away. . . . Positively couldn't! Well, and then we had to walk back. Say, I don't care much about promenading when I am tied to a horse's tail. And the beggar of a horse did run, I can tell you—and I behind it—because I was tied to its tail, see?"

"Silence!" commanded the sergeant. "No talking here."

When the formalities of the surrender were over, the six deserters (I was one of the guard who escorted them with fixed bayonets) were marched off to prison.

The keys rattled. The sergeant of the guard considered it necessary to give vent to his bad humour in many superfluous remarks about "the dirty, ragged, good-for-nothing lot of *poumpistes*, whom the penal battalion would soon cure of skinning out," and gave Rader, who was the last to cross the cell's threshold, a mighty kick. Rader fell at full length. Then the heavy door swung to behind them. . . .

A few years ago Herr von Rader and his companions would have been sentenced to quite a curious kind of punishment which was at that time considered in the Foreign Legion to be a radical cure for deserters—a kind of mediaeval torture which, by the way, was not kept for deserters solely, but came into use very often. This was the "silo" and the *crapaudine*.

The silo consisted of a funnel-shaped hole in the ground, broad at the top and pointed towards the bottom. A regular funnel. Into this hole, used as a cell for solitary confinement, the misdoers would be thrown, clad only in a thin suit of fatigue clothes, without a blanket or any protection at all against the rain or against the sun, at the mercy of the heat by day and the cold by night. The poor devils would be left for several days in this "prison." They could not lie down, for the bottom part of the hole was only one or two feet square. They spent day and night alternately standing and crouching, now in pouring rain, now in the burning sun. They very soon became ill from the foul vapours. When at length they were taken out of the silo, they could neither walk nor stand and had to be carried into hospital. Now and then a silo prisoner died in his hole.

They say in the Foreign Legion that it was General de Négrier who abolished the silo. When he was inspecting Saida, he found a row of fifteen silos, one beside the other, and every single one occupied.

He had the unfortunates taken out and they fell down in a dead faint on coming into the fresh air. Thereupon the general had every one of the silos filled up before his own eyes and forbade the silo penalty ever being used again.

A more primitive but perhaps a still more brutal torture was the *crapaudine*. The man to be punished was simply tied up into a bundle and thrown into a corner, his hands and feet being tied together on his back, till they formed a sort of semicircle. Such a *crapaudinaire* lay there helpless day and night, totally unable to move. The most he could do when he tried very hard was to roll from one side to the other. For a quarter of an hour a day he would be set free and got bread to eat and water to drink. A day and a night in the *crapaudine* was enough to deprive a man of the use of his limbs—several days gave him his *quietus*.

This penalty has also been abolished. It exists still in a milder form. In the field and on the march an offender is often punished by being bound to two posts driven into the ground.

Today, (at time of first publication), the punishments in the Legion are not quite as cruel as they once were. At any rate their cruelty is not quite so apparent. Rader's friends got off with fourteen days' prison, while he himself, after waiting in prison an age for his trial, was sentenced by court-martial. The poor fellow had lost his cap and belt and got a year's penal servitude for "theft of equipment." What happened to him there I have never heard.

There is no fixed penalty for desertion. In general the *poump-istes* are treated pretty mildly and sentenced, when they happen to be recruits, to 40 to 120 days' prison. Only when they are recruits. The veterans are always brought before the court-martial. But this is merely the general rule; if, for instance, a deserter has managed to get for some reason or another into the sergeant's or some other non-commissioned officer's "black books," the charge against him will be certain to include the loss of some part of his uniform, even when this is not in the least the case. The Foreign Legion has its own ideas of the subjects of pains and penalties.

Viewed from the surface of things, there actually is a sort of scale of punishment. At the beginning comes extra *corvée*, which is quite bad enough. For little omissions in the daily routine, for a *paquetage* not quite accurately put together, or for a button not polished well enough, the offender can be sentenced by the sergeant of his section to perform the heavy duties of the *corvée*, while his comrades are making their repairs or having instructions. As long as I served in the Legion I was never punished for a fault of my own, not even with extra *corvée*—I took good care not to give the slightest excuse for punishment. More than once, however, I made the acquaintance of general *corvée*. This was our sergeant's speciality. When he inspected our quarters in the morning and found some petty excuse for finding fault, he did not bother with details, but just said:

"Eh, corporal! A dirty, nasty room! Disgusting! The whole lot of you extra *corvée* this afternoon, under your supervision, corporal!"

Whereupon the corporal cursed and every fellow in the room anathematised the sergeant as a "*sale cochon*"—a filthy swine. As the "swine," however, was clothed with the bristles of authority, the extra *corvée* had to be performed in spite of all curses and anathemas.

Pretty nearly as frequent as this was confinement to barracks. This comes next in the scale of punishments and is always connected with *salle de police*. *Salle de police* is only another name for the general cells in the prisons. Above all the offenders are not allowed to leave the barracks in their spare time. In other respects they do their duty as usual. When their day's work is finished, however, at five o'clock, they are called out every half-hour and sometimes every quarter of an hour to the drill-ground, where their names are called over by the sergeant of the guard.

Anyone who happens to miss one of these roll-calls finds himself in prison for a week. In their fear of not hearing the signal the men have not a single minute's quiet, and can hardly find time to clean their kit for the morrow. At nine o'clock, at the evening roll-call, they must report themselves in the guard-room, and are shut up in the *salle de police* for the nigh— in the general cells, which are filled to overflowing. Sleep among the crush of men and in that nauseating atmosphere is only possible for a few hours, when the tired body demands its right in spite of the disgusting surroundings. Next morning at five they are dismissed and have to perform the usual routine work with the rest of the company. Eight days' *salle de police* are looked upon as a very light punishment—a sure sign that the average *légionnaire*'s susceptibilities are not all too fine.

Salle de police was something quite in the ordinary run of affairs for us: confinement to barracks was a part of life in the Legion. In our quarters I was the only man who had not made its acquaintance, and that was the merest chance, luck plain and simple.

No one excited himself about extra *corvée* and confinement to barracks. Every single man in the Legion had, however, a mighty respect for the prison.

Prison, arrest in the regimental lock-up, is the Legion's real punishment. Imprisonment in the Legion is made up of the hardest work possible, and living under the most awful sanitary conditions; one can only form an idea of what this punishment is like when one has had a look at the Legion's prisons.[1]

Next comes *cellule*, solitary confinement on starvation diet.

Then come the *Zephyrs*, those condemned to the penal battalion. Every two or three weeks a transport of *Zephyrs* left the barracks in old ragged uniforms. In the battalion itself they have to wear the coffee-brown clothes of the convict.

"The sections for the reformation of incorrigibles" is the official name for this battalion, and deportation to the *Zephyrs* is the severest punishment which can be put into execution without the authority of a court-martial. The official grasp of the meaning of the word incorrigible is, however, a trifle strange sometimes. Under the strictest surveillance these unfortunates carry on pioneer work in the far south. They make roads, they dig wells, they build new stations in the most unhealthy parts of Algeria, far removed from all civilisation. They have to work as even a *légionnaire*, to whom the hardest work is so familiar, would only work under the sternest compulsion. And if extra pioneer work is needed in the south, if, for instance, a new road is to be built, the battalion's numbers increase with amazing rapidity. It is really astonishing how the number of incorrigibles in the Legion increases just when the military administration needs men—for work!

"*Much work—many Zephyrs!*" says the Legion's proverb.

The scale finishes with the heavy military punishments, from penal servitude to the death sentence, and here the decision of the Algerian court-martial in Oran is final. Its sentences are renowned for their pitiless severity. To be brought before this court-martial the *légionnaire* need not have committed any very grave offence. It is enough if he has lost some part of his uniform.

In a well-known French historical work on the subject of the Foreign Legion, Roger de Beauvoir writes:

> Each of the two discipline sections is 150 men strong: of these 300, 200 at least are in the penal section for selling part of their kit. It used to be the custom to 'let the stomach pay' for this offence, *i.e.*, the offender was put on bread and water till he had

---

1. See close of chapter.

replaced the lost equipment from the mess allowance that was saved. This punishment was finally considered too barbarously old-fashioned, and the court-martial took its place, which passes sentence of six months' imprisonment. The *légionnaires* long for the old *régime*!

And thereby hangs a tale.

A very sad story, too. . . . No sensible man will attempt to dispute the fact that iron discipline is essential for the lurid mixture of human material in the Legion. If the justice of the Foreign Legion was in practice what it is in theory—stern but just—one could not say a word against it. It is, however, only just in theory, in the intention of the military law-makers. In reality it is the justice of unlimited tyranny; made so by the individual tyranny of officers and non-commissioned officers in individual cases, and in general by an obstinate tenacity to the letter of the law.

Every French officer and every French court-martial acts under the time-honoured assumption that the *légionnaire* makes a brave soldier, but is in all other respects a thoroughbred rogue and knave, and that one cannot go far wrong in assuming the worst about him. The word of a superior is always accepted as proof of guilt. There is no better illustration of this than the everlasting heavy penalties which are meted out for "theft of equipment." This sort of theft exists, of course. Theft is not a thing to be very much wondered at when the men's wages are five *centimes* a day.

But many hundreds of innocents are punished for this offence in the course of a year.

The favourite trick of non-commissioned officers, when they have a spite against a man, is to inspect his kit suddenly. Some trifle or other, a tie or a couple of straps, are quite sure to be missing and then there is the *casus belli!* "Lost is stolen—sold!" "Thus the axiom of the Legion's authorities, against which the most positive assertions are of no avail. Now and then an offender of this sort is leniently treated, and let off by the regiment with sixty days' imprisonment; in the majority of cases, however, he is tried by the court-martial.

A typical case: "Jean the Unlucky" was the nickname of a young Frenchman in my company who had been sentenced in his second year of service to six months in the penal section for stealing a sash. He swore he was innocent, and as far as I can tell he spoke the truth, as his mother sent him twenty *francs* every month. Thus he was quite well off according to Foreign Legion ideas, and certainly need not have risked a heavy penalty by selling his *ceinture* for a few *sous*. The probabilities were in favour of his innocence, but that did not help him. He was sentenced. He survived his six months in the hell of the penal battalion and was then sent back to his company.

And now his troubles really began. At the time of his trial he had, in his rage at the false accusation, made more than one biting remark about our adjutant and his little ways. This the colour-sergeant never forgot. In spite of the fact that Little Jean was a quiet fellow, who did his duty to the best of his ability, a good soldier and a capital shot, he kept wandering backwards and forwards between the prison and the company, the company and the prison. Nothing he could do was right. Sometimes his boots were not properly cleaned, sometimes his bed was a centimetre out of the dead straight line in which beds must stand, and at another time he had not stood properly at attention at roll-call. Such were Little Jean's grave offences against the holy spirit of the Legion's discipline—ridiculous accusations, which bore the stamp of spite so plainly that even our careless captain should have noticed it.

These human machines punished automatically, without feeling, without thinking for an instant. The sergeant's reports demanding punishment for Little Jean's awful sins were signed automatically. When the sergeant put him down for eight days' confinement to barracks, the captain mechanically increased the penalty to eight days' imprisonment, because *Jean le malheureux*, coming from the penal section, had naturally a very bad reputation. Then came the commander of the battalion, who, not caring to be outdone in matters of discipline, doubled the dose. The sergeant's modest eight days' confinement to barracks had now grown to sixteen days' imprisonment.

But now came the embodiment of authority in the regiment in the person of the colonel. This colonel had his own ideas as to how one should treat the pernicious elements in the regiment:

Second-class soldier Jean Dubois, No. 14892, 11th company, is sentenced by the colonel to 40 days' imprisonment for continued slackness and insubordination.

That was read to us the next time the regimental orders came out.

You see, the machine worked admirably. Its mechanism runs with wonderful accuracy. Anyone who took an interest in the matter could work the whole thing out in advance. Dubois did this. He knew well enough what was waiting for him—from day to day he became quieter, from day to day sadder, so that at length he hardly spoke at all to his comrades. He could do nothing to protect himself; he hadn't even enough energy left for flight. Good Lord, he had long lost that little bit of energy he had, lost it—somewhere down south in the sunburnt wastes, where the penal battalion works and suffers.

The machinery ground on. . . . Eighty days' imprisonment was Little Jean's next dose. After that he got sixty days' *cellule*—just for a change. If you consider only the number of days, you might think he had got off pretty cheaply this time. Not a bit of it. These sixty days were days of starvation. For *cellule* means hunger and emaciation—awful hunger and awful emaciation.

After his sixty days of diet cure Dubois came back to the company for just a week, if I remember rightly. Then the machine began to work again. This time it was a month he got. . . Thirty days' imprisonment—for this incorrigible and insubordinate subject! No, one really cannot be surprised that the colonel lost all patience. So he refused to confirm the punishment and sent the black sheep of the company to trial by court-martial. And once more the machine began to do its work.

Two years' imprisonment, two years' penal servitude in a fortress, for *Jean le malheureux!*

With the next batch of convicts they carried him off to Oran. I have heard nothing of him since—I do not know how he fared as a convict. In my unconquerable optimism I am ready to assume that this two years' interregnum did not do particular harm to Little Jean's health and that he returned home, having done his duty by the Foreign Legion, dapper and cheerful as he used to be. Even this supposition gives us a very pretty bit of arithmetic.

Jean Dubois' original period of service	5 years
Extra service for time spent in the penal battalion	6 months
Ditto for regimental punishments	7 months
Ditto for imprisonment in fortress	2 years
	———
Total time Jean Dubois had to serve in place of his original five years	8 years 1 month

In this optimistic piece of arithmetic my optimism even goes so far as to assume that Jean the Unlucky, during his two years of imprisonment and during the rest of his period of service, did not incur any additional penalties.

If I, however, compel myself to consider his career from a pessimistic point of view, the sum works out much more prettily. Dubois had not a very strong constitution and it is quite possible that the penal battalion, plus imprisonment, plus starvation, plus despair, quite finished him off. In that case the loss of a blue scarf, a spiteful sergeant and the crass stupidity of a series of officers have been the death of him.

But if Jean Dubois really got over his years of prison—when he returns home (he is a Frenchman!) his strength will not be worth much in the workaday world.

While I think of it. There is yet another very pretty piece of arithmetic. Little Jean was a thoughtful man. When he comes back home after his long years of Legion he will perhaps sit down and work out how much he has earned in these eight, long, hard years.

The example would look like this:

	Francs
First year of service, 5 *centimes* a day	18.25
Second year of service, 5 *centimes* a day	18.25
Third year of service, 5 *centimes* a day	18.25
Fourth year of service, 10 *centimes* a day	36.50
Fifth year of service, 10 *centimes* a day	36.50
Grand Total	127.75

The other three years? In these Little Jean worked free, *gratis*, for nothing. These three years were *rabiau*, as they say in the Legion, of no use, superfluous. In his three *rabiau* years Little Jean naturally got no pay. Why should a convict get paid?

So you see Little Jean's earnings amounted to the grand total of 127 *francs* 75 *centimes*—earned in eight years. Besides all this, this worthless fellow had been fed all this time! And clothed into the bargain.

Yes—*c'est la Légion!*

The prison in the barracks at Sidi-bel-Abbès used always to loom before me like a threatening spectre.

On both sides of the entrance to the barracks, close to the road, but separated from it by a high wall, lay the two little houses with their flat tin roofs which caught the sun's rays so pitilessly. Inside there were rows and rows of cell doors in the long narrow corridors. The single cells were a little more than three yards long and one yard broad; the general cells were perhaps five yards square. There was no light, and a little hole in the wall and an opening over the door were the sole means of ventilation. The floor was flagged or of clay. There was a wooden bench in each cell, a water-jug, and an old tin pail.

The single cells and the general cells were exactly alike in their "fittings"—whether five men or fifty were shut up in these cells made no difference! They got, according to the regulations, one water-jug and one pail! I was never (and even today that is a satisfaction to me) shut up in the Legion's prison. But I have seen enough, when I was on guard there, to have had quite enough of the prison without any nearer experience of it.

I repeat: five yards square, thirty, forty, or more occupants: an air-hole nine inches in diameter high up in the walls and a tiny crack over the door.

Any of these cells would at once be condemned by a veterinary as unfit even for a pigsty!

Before *réveillé* at five o'clock in the morning all the sentries on guard were marched up to the prison, and the sergeant opened the cells, whereupon an awful stench streamed out. He read out the names from the prison register, and the prisoners came out of the cells into the passage as their names were called. Then they began to clean up. The pails were carried by two men, accompanied by a sentry, to the sewer openings in the barrack-yard. When the bigger cells were over-filled (and this was almost always the case) they looked awful. The room was like a sewer, flooded, pestilential. . . . To clean the cells there were only a couple of old brooms in the prison. A few pails of water were flooded over the floor, carelessly and hurriedly, for the sergeants did not care about wasting too much time on the *prisonniers*. A little water and a few strokes with the broom! What is not washed away trickles through the cracks and crannies in the stone floor and forms a new basis for pestilence.

The bowl of black coffee which forms the *légionnaire's* breakfast is not given to the prisoners. They get no breakfast. They are allowed to wash themselves at the basin in the corridor. Then they are led out to work, on an empty stomach, frozen through by the chilly African night spent uncovered on a hard wooden bench, and faint from breathing in that pestilential atmosphere.

All those who were sentenced to short terms of imprisonment were commandeered to clean up the barrack-yard, to split wood, and to break stones. The prisoners with longer sentences, and those in

151

cellule, had to go out to the "march of punishment," marching round in a small circle for two hours on end, carrying heavy bags of sand, now and then doubling for the sake of variety. When the corporal in command was in bad temper he made them go through a course of Swedish gymnastics into the bargain. This was tremendous work when burdened with the heavy sack, and it strained the muscles and nerves in a way that nothing else could.

At ten o'clock the prisoners were given soup. They never got full rations, since as long as they were in prison their mess allowance ceased as well as their pay.

The soup is thin, and the piece of meat which swims in it is as small as may be. . . . Their bread rations consist of half of what they get in the company. The prisoners in solitary confinement are placed on starvation diet. Their soup consists of hot water with little bits of potatoes and bread-crusts, and they only get this every other day. In the interval they have to live on bread—on a quarter of the Legion's bread rations. One must have seen how terribly emaciated these poor fellows become in a few days to be able to do justice to the barbarity of a system which has three main ideas: undernourishment, overwork, frightful sanitary conditions.

After they have finished "dinner," their work begins again. The drill suits had got dirty, and bore signs of the nights they had gone through. The operation, too, of emptying the tin pails cannot be performed without the suits being considerably the worse for it. But the drill suits were only changed when an inspection by the colonel was imminent, and clean underclothes were a luxury absolutely unknown in prison.

The sergeants on guard always considered it an important part of their duties to treat the prisoners as badly as possible. In the prison it simply rained curses. Many sergeants took an especial delight in inspecting the prisoners every three hours throughout the night. They had to come out into the yard, and the sergeant read their names and numbers by the light of the lantern, taking as long about it as he could, while the poor wretches had to stand there motionless in their thin clothes for half an hour in the cold night air. This would be repeated three or four times a night. In this way the sergeant manages to while away his dreary night on guard, and had in addition the pleasing sense of having played his little part in the regiment's system of justice. Under discipline in the Foreign Legion they understand a series of variations, improvements or otherwise, on the mediaeval systems of torture.

It is merely the petty offences against discipline that are punished in these hovels.

I was on the watch in the narrow corridor of one of these prisons, pacing to and fro on the cold flags with fixed bayonet. Eight hours before the *poumpistes*, Rader and the rest of them, had been brought in. Through the narrow opening between the wall and the prison, a little strip of starlit sky could be seen, and down the narrow passage the cold night wind howled. But it could not drive away the pestilential stench which hung heavy over the prison and which was perpetually being increased by the vapours from the ventilation holes and the tiny openings in the cellules. This awful smell tortured my nerves and rendered sentry-go in the prison anything but pleasant.

Besides Rader and his fellow-deserters, there were forty others in the general cell. When at ten o'clock at night the sergeant inspected the prison and the cells were opened, I saw how the men lay huddled together on the wooden benches, man to man, like sardines packed in a tin. But in spite of this scarcely twenty out of the forty prisoners could find room on the bench.

The others crouched in the corners, sleeping with their knees drawn up to their chins; several lay on the bare floor, filthy though it was. It was freezing cold for them in their thin drill clothes. The prison blankets they had been given were hardly worth calling blankets, ancient rags, so thin that one could see through them like a veil and so small that the men had the choice of covering their feet or their bodies; the blankets were not big enough to do both. They were stiff with dirt and most of them were alive with vermin. In the daytime they were just thrown into a corner of the cell.

It was no wonder that the men who had just been shut up in this cell could not sleep. Once I heard Rader ask gently who was doing sentry. He must have stood on the shoulders of one of his comrades to be able to reach the ventilation hole, which was high up in the wall. When I answered it was I, he said he could not stand it anymore in there—hadn't I a cigarette? I spitted a packet of cigarettes on my bayonet and handed it up to him.

"Keep up your pecker, old man," I whispered.

"Good Lord, good Lord . . ." was the reply, in a pitiful tone which hadn't even a touch of Rader's droll humour left in it.

The sound of groans and curses reached me continually from the cell; all spoke very gently for they knew that they would be severely punished if a noise was heard. It is a prison custom for the sentry in the corridor to let the butt of his rifle fall loudly on the floor when he hears the sergeant coming. This is a warning signal. When in their excitement they spoke a little louder I could now and then hear through the opening what they were saying. In eloquent French, one of the prisoners, whose accent proclaimed him to be a man of education, was complaining of life in the Legion, and all was still in the cell while the ringing voice spoke in passionate excitement.

Snatches of what I heard are still fixed in my memory:

"My God, if I could only die!—My friends, I've always done my duty here.—I've marched and marched and marched for four long years.—For four years I've borne burdens, exposed to wind and weather, and have tired my strength. Four long years! Yes, I've lost my tie, *oh, la la*, a thin blue rag worth a couple of *centimes*—and was marched off to prison! I'd stolen the tie, I'd sold it—who believes the word of a *légionnaire*! *Mea culpa*, my friends!"

"*Mea maxima culpa!* "repeated the speaker quietly. "'Tis true one has never been much use and has made a monstrous thing of one's life—you and I and all of us! And why not? That's all past and done with now. All the same—I'm ashamed of the country in which the Foreign Legion can exist. I'm a Frenchman. But I say: Damn the Legion, damn the land of the Legion. . . ."

And over all there hung the pestilential vapours in the tiny room with the crowded humanity within.

When I was relieved at midnight the sergeant asked: "Anything unusual?"

"No, nothing special," I answered.

CHAPTER 13

Some Types of Vice

It was always a marvel to me that neither cards nor dice played the slightest part in the life of the Legion, in sharp contrast with the important part they take in the life of the English Tommy, and especially of the American soldier, who is an incorrigible gambler. On a little station in Texas a detachment of sly old regulars in the course of the single night that they were quartered there cleaned out all the cowboys of the neighbourhood. I was one of the victims. But that's another story. . . . Anyhow, the Legion is free from the vice of gambling. This is perhaps hardly to be wondered at; five *centimes* wages. The possibility of winning or losing five *centimes* is hardly worth a throw of the dice.

In its place all the vices of almost every nation in the world can be found in the Foreign Legion. This is not saying too much; I've looked on.

Vicious influences are, however, much stronger in Indo-China and in French Tonquin, where the garrisons of the various stations are all drawn from the Legion. Veterans like Smith used to tell me things about the life in Tonquin that almost made my hair stand on end. In the inland districts the stations are quite small, and a few *légionnaires* have to look after a large number of natives. The entire system of justice on such a station, including the power of life and death, lies in the hands of a couple of young officers and a few sergeants and corporals. Surrounded by all possible human vices in their very worst forms, to whose influence the deadly monotony inevitable on one of these stations is added, the men live exposed to constant danger occasioned both by the intrigues among the natives and the murderous climate. The one seeks relief in spirits, the other swears by opium.

The fact that opium-smoking plays an important part in the life of the French Navy and among the French Army officers in the Colonies has been made public often enough already: every veteran in the Legion knows well enough that in Toulon and Marseilles there are countless opium dens which depend solely on the custom of French officers. These opium dens were thoroughly discussed in the French press during the trial of the midshipman Ullmo.

The habit of opium-smoking has, in nearly all cases, been acquired in Indo-China. Spirits, opium, and loneliness form the fruitful soil in which the Legion's vice takes root. In solitary cases even the officers come under its influence. When this happens the results are sometimes very terrible. . . .

Among the garrisons of Indo-China the most notorious used to be those of Sui-can and Bac-le.

A certain Lieutenant Duchesne, who was later killed in battle, many say by his own men, and the fact that the bullet hit him in the back goes to prove the truth of this statement, has made his name immortal in the Legion in this connection. Though he has been dead several years, one still hears of his cruelty. His *légionnaires* were all forced to submit themselves to his vicious freaks, resistance being punished with the penal section, which is ten times worse in Tonquin than those in Algeria. The obedient, however, were promoted.

Even today, (at time of first publication), the same sort of thing can be found here and there in Indo-China. There are always stories like this to be heard in the Legion, adjutants and *sous*-officiers being freely named who are said to owe their promotion to the vicious preference of some officer or other. A good deal is perhaps spiteful gossip, but the stories are so frequent, and the details given are so minute, that there must be a certain amount of truth in them.

In addition to these outside influences, a further cause of depravity is the involuntary celibacy to which the *légionnaire* is subjected. And this celibacy has its origin in a financial consideration: the five *centimes* per day.

. . . . One always comes back again to the same point from which one started.

Whoever really knows the Foreign Legion, whoever takes the trouble to probe the depths of its misery and sin, of its brutality and vice, always comes back, like a man walking in a circle, to the same source of all its ills: the pitiful wage that's not worth calling a wage which this business enterprise pays: this infamous business enterprise that a chivalrous nation has so long tolerated and tolerates still.

All human vices are to be found in the Legion. And first among the minor ones comes drunkenness. This takes the first place, occurring most frequently and being the most characteristic and easily indulged, in a country where the price of a litre of heavy wine varies between ten and twenty *centimes*.

Das ist ja eben das Malheur:
Wer Sorgen hat, trinkt auch Likör.

"*The man who has troubles, drinks*"—Algerian wine, or in Indo-China a horrible spirit, which is distilled, I believe, from rice and which rejoices in the name of "*Shum-Shum*," and has the advantage of an uncommonly high percentage of alcohol. It has only one drawback, and that is its infernal smell, which delicate European noses cannot stand. The *légionnaire*, however, drinks it: while drinking he holds his nose, since he hardly values its aroma as he does its alcohol. I have often heard old *légionnaires* singing the praises of *Shum-Shum*. One could get accustomed to its smell, they said, and it made one very, very drunk.

The droll verses of the old German humorist, Wilhelm Busch, with their subtle point, might have been written for the Legion. How they drank in the canteen of the Foreign Legion in Sidi-bel-Abbès. The litre—a litre of wine—took the place of the current coinage. Thus it was nothing unusual for a *légionnaire*, when asked to wash for a comrade well endowed with this world's goods, to raise one finger: that meant, of course, a litre.

"If we hadn't wine. . . ." I shall never forget Smith's pet expression.

There are no statistics on this point. I am, however, quite certain that a good half of the miserable wages paid to the Foreign Legion are spent in purchasing the red wine of Algiers. In addition to this, nine-tenths, nay ninety-nine-hundredths of the notes and postal orders which the *légionnaires* are continuously sent by anxious parents and relations in Europe go to swell the coffers of *Madame la Cantinière*.

This is in no sense an accusation. When one considers the life of the soldier of the Legion with understanding, one recognises that no one in the world has more cares than he, no one a better right to his few hours of oblivion. Yes, the African *légionnaire* has a hard life, and drunkenness in his case is really almost excusable. I only want to show what a prominent *rôle* the red wine of Algeria does play in the life of the Legion. It is, it is true, the most general vice, but it is the only means of obtaining a few moments of bliss, and the sole source of pleasure.

Wine is the cause of a great many punishments. Drunkenness is a "sale offense," to use the soldier's expression, a dishonourable offence that is severely punished, and which continually furnishes the penal section with new material.

As an instance of this I will give you the story of a man in my company, a Belgian named Lascelles. At regular intervals he got a postal order for a small sum sent him from some relative in Europe. On receiving his money, he vanished as soon as he came off duty and did not come back to the barracks again for at least twenty-four hours. As long as his coppers lasted, he used to go from wine-shop to wine-shop and empty bottle after bottle. On his return he would be immediately locked up for overstaying his leave of absence; generally, however, to celebrate the event he had made a great disturbance, and committed a series of more or less grave offences, for each of which he was punished singly.

Every month the time he spent in prison grew longer and longer, beginning with a trifling eight days and increasing to a month's solitary confinement. In between whiles, Lascelles was a capital soldier, who did his work willingly enough. When, however, his name was read out at roll-call—a postal order for Lascelles—one could be sure that a day later would find him in prison once more. In a few months he had worked his way up the regimental scale of punishments, and then came the inevitable end and he was sent off to the penal section.

Lascelles' misfortunes were at any rate his own fault. It often happens, however, that spiteful sergeants in the Legion take advantage of a man's love of drink to work his ruin.

A sergeant has a spite against a man and waits patiently for the day when he comes into the barracks in a state of intoxication. He then follows him to his quarters and gives him some order or other. The man feels how needless and spiteful this is, and, being hardly in a condition to think of danger, answers with a curse. This is just what is wanted. Even when the man is sober enough to do what he has been ordered, he is severely punished for his curse. Should he continue to be "insubordinate "he comes before the court-martial.

This is a very old trick in the Legion, and only recruits or very old *légionnaires* under the influence of drink and suffering at the same time from the *cafard* are caught by it. The average *légionnaire* is careful, and, drunk or sober, obeys every order no matter how furious he may be. "*Nix Zephyrs pour moi*," he says.

"Ah yes, there is another side to the proverb, "If there were no wine. . . . .""

Every vice was represented there. The most brutal egotism and boundless avarice ruled that hard life. One grudged one's comrade a crust of bread, a sip of wine, or a piece of meat. The man who had a few shillings sent him was an object of hate and envy.

Intrigue—slander—lying—theft—the Legion brings all the bad points in a man's character to full development.

Whose fault is it?

CHAPTER 14

My Escape

The days came and the days went, and with every day I understood more what it meant to be a *légionnaire* in Africa.

The knowledge so gained was not pleasant.

One day I was on guard in the Arab prison of Sidi-bel-Abbès, an ugly, gloomy building in the middle of the town. An old retired sergeant of the Legion was overseer of the Arab prison, and with the help of two gendarmes kept the Arab prisoners in strictest order. The prison was always crowded with native sinners, for the petty thefts in the market-place and the constant fights in the negro quarter kept the cells of that grey building near the Place Sadi Carnot always full. The native prisoners had often made trouble, and mutinies had been quite frequent. The last outbreak had been very serious, so since that time the Legion had sent a guard every day to the Arab prison consisting of a corporal and six men.

My rifle with fixed bayonet over my shoulder, I kept pacing slowly on the top of the broad wall surrounding the prison in an enormous square. The sun burned down pitilessly. In the tiny courtyard small groups of Arab prisoners cowered in the sulky silence of inactivity. All talking was forbidden in the prison. The overseer's sharp words of command now and then, and the ring of my steps on the stones of the wall, sounded into the silence. Mechanically I followed the path pre-scribed for "sentry-go," marching round and round the prison square.

From the high wall I had a view of all Sidi-bel-Abbès. The town was like a city of the dead in this frightful heat. The blinds in all the houses were pulled down and there was not a soul to be seen in the streets. In the hot, trembling air the faint outlines of the mountains of Thessala glittered in the far distance. There was not a breath of wind.

Two *légionnaires* in white fatigue uniforms turned into the street leading to the prison. They were men from our company, bringing us our evening soup. They called out something to me that I could not understand and I acknowledged it with an indifferent nod. Then they knocked at the gate of the prison and had to wait an age till the overseer opened it with his jingling bunch of keys and they could carry their soup-pail into the guard-room. Some minutes later one of them came into the yard by the guard-room and beckoned to me to come nearer to him. As I approached, I saw that he held a white something in his hand.

"*Eh, une lettre pour toi!*" he cried. "Here's a letter for you."

Very much annoyed I called down to him to hurry up and get out of this. It was too hot for practical jokes. I never got letters. . . .

"But here is one," said the man. "Your name, your company, your number—everything all right! *La la*—I'm off—I'll give your letter to the corporal. May Allah better your bad temper! *Sapristi*, how hot it is!"

I had to wait half an hour until I was relieved. Those were terrible minutes. A letter a letter for me? It seemed almost impossible. There was nobody in the world who could or should know where I was or what I was doing. The blood rose in hot waves to my head—and all at once I recognised that there was only one human being who could have written to me—that her love was not dead.

Slowly the seconds, the minutes went by. I waited in indescribable suspense. The sun was sinking. The houses of Sidi-bel-Abbès were bathed in its ruddy glow. Below me in the prison yard I heard a noisy chattering in guttural Arabic. The prisoners were being given their food and were then allowed to speak. The poor devils' chatter seemed to pierce my brain; that buzzing noise down below hurt me, until I could not stand it any longer.

"Be quiet there!" I cried.

There was immediate silence. A *gendarme* called out to me that I had made a mistake and that talking was allowed. "*Pas défendu de parler*," he said to the prisoners, and the Arabs looked up at me with angry eyes.

And I had to go on waiting, waiting. . . .

This awful suspense seemed to have lasted for hours when the corporal at last came to relieve me. The conventionality of passing orders and sentry instructions was being gone through; we were on service and it was contrary to all discipline—but I could not wait any longer.

"You've a letter for me, corporal?" I asked.

"Yes, there is a letter for you," he answered. "You can have it as soon as I have done relieving the sentries. *En avant—marche!*"

A new period of anxious waiting and torturing expectation. . . . At last the corporal of the guard came back and put his hand in his pocket:

"*Voila!*"

On the white envelope I saw the characters of the handwriting I knew so well. I went out into the square which was now empty, as the prisoners had been locked up in their cells again. I read and read— again and again. . . .

Love stretched out its hand to the lost soldier of the Legion and spoke to him of happiness to come. Long years hence when the *légionnaire* would be no longer a *légionnaire.* The letter's many pages bore traces of tears. I wanted to tear off my uniform, that brand of slavery condemning me to inactivity. Within me all was in a whirl. In the darkness of the ugly court I dreamed dreams of the past and hopes of the future so hopelessly far off. During the four hours from watch to watch I sat motionless in the prison-yard.

In these few hours there came to me that energy which meant the beginning of a new life. Then it was my turn for sentry duty again. And then I sat down at the small table in the guard-room while the corporal and the other men slept, and wrote an endless letter with the corporal's pencil on the back of report forms. Page upon page. . . .

The next day a letter from my mother came; a letter that neither asked questions nor held reproaches. It only spoke of love and anxiety for me. This letter solved the riddle of how my whereabouts had been discovered. After long months of waiting and wondering the people who loved me got the idea that I might be in the Foreign Legion, since the last letter they received from me had been dated from the French fortress, Belfort. My mother wrote to the general in command of the fortress and to the French Secretary of War. The answer was long delayed, but at last the news came that I had joined the Foreign Legion at Sidi-bel-Abbès—that I was the *légionnaire* number 17889!

With that hour in the Arab prison which brought me the first letter, the days of suffering began. I performed my duty and did my work like a machine, thinking of nothing but the letters which the next post would bring me. I hardly spoke a word to anybody in those times. When I was off duty I went for long walks in the still paths by the fortifications in order to be alone. Finally only one idea governed my thoughts: Flight!

Week after week I received letters every day, begging and beseeching me to have patience. I was to remember that all hopes for the future would be shattered if I was caught deserting. Better to wait for years than to risk everything. But I could not wait. And one day there came a registered letter from my mother. When I opened it, I held banknotes for a large sum of money in my hand. . . .

This meant freedom! I crossed the court of the barracks as one in a dream. This money in my pocket meant new life for me—my mother had for the second time given me life. I knew what a sacrifice this money meant; how hard it must have been for my mother with her tiny widow's pension to scrape together such a sum of money for me. And all at once a wave of happiness overcame me—I should be free! I should be able to thank those loving ones who were helping me. . . .

I got that letter at five o'clock in the afternoon. I was just off duty and had come back to the barracks, having been pulling out weeds in the Legion's cemetery. That should be my last bit of work as *légionnaire*.

Not a single hour I intended to wait. There was no more rest for me in the land of Sidi-bel-Abbès. In our quarters my comrades were sitting at supper as I came back from the regimental *post-bureau*, and Smith was much surprised at my eating nothing, and at my putting on at once my extra uniform. He looked suspiciously at me, as if he had an idea that I had something out of the way on my mind. I would have been only too glad to say a last goodbye to the old bugler who had been a true friend to me in his rough way, but he was sitting at table with the rest of the men. When I had finished dressing and had quietly taken my letters and the few trifles I wanted to take with me out of my knapsack, Smith came up and lay down on his bed as usual after supper.

"Goodbye, old man," I whispered. "You've been a good fellow."

Smith did not move. Only his eyes lighted up. . . .

"Got money?" he asked gently.

"Yes."

"Then it's all right. Goodbye, sonny—goodbye!"

As I went out the other men were sitting on the benches doing the various odd jobs which were part of life in the Legion. They rubbed and polished—polished and rubbed. At that time they were hardly more to me than a passer-by in the street. Now, I confess, the face of every one of them is indelibly burnt into my brain.

I was to be subjected to a final annoyance.

The sergeant of the guard stopped me at the gate of the barracks, because in my excitement I had buttoned up my overcoat on the wrong side. He said he had a good mind to turn me back for my carelessness.

"*Nom de Dieu!* you pig, don't you know that this month the overcoats are buttoned on the right side?"

But he let me go. Through the crowd of *légionnaires* I hurried down the promenade. The first place I had to go to was the *Credit Lyonnais*, the famous French bank which had a branch in Sidi-bel-Abbès near the Place Sadi Carnot. The greater part of my money consisted of Belgian banknotes, which naturally were not in circulation in Algeria, and I thought I should be able to have them changed at the bank more quickly and cheaply than anywhere else.

There I made a mistake. The clerk at the counter explained in a roundabout way that Belgian banknotes were of no use to them, and that it would cost a lot of money to send them to Paris. He was only greedy, of course (everybody in Sidi-bel-Abbès is), and trying to get an especially high commission out of me. Perhaps he thought that a *légionnaire* should be too pleased at having so much money to bother about a few *francs* more or less. There he was in error. I replied I should complain to the colonel of my regiment that the only bank in Sidi-bel-Abbès tried to overcharge a simple soldier. Whereupon this greedy clerk of a world-famous bank grumblingly took my notes and gave me French money for them.

Through the brightly illuminated main streets, saluting officers right and left, I hurried to the Ghetto. In the very first alley of the Ghetto I met an old fellow who looked promising. I tapped him on the shoulder.

"Eh! Civilian clothes?"

The Jew raised his forefinger warningly.

"Can't sell to *légionnaires*."

I turned on my heels and went slowly on. But he was after me already.

"How much?"

"Twenty *francs*."

"Fifty!"

"Thirty."

"Forty-five!"

"Look here," I said. (The conversation was held in bad Algerian

French, of course.) "I'll give you forty *francs*, and that settles it. But I've got to have those clothes quick."

The Jew looked at me dubiously, and held out the palms of his hands. One could not be mistaken about the gesture: he had his doubts about my solvency. So I reassured the old man by showing him a few gold pieces. Now the son of Israel was quite satisfied, and led me a few steps farther on into a house. A tiny little lamp was smoking in a foul-smelling room.

"Sarah!" called out my companion.

An old woman came hobbling out of a neighbouring room, and when she heard what was wanted went off and fetched a heap of clothes. Amongst them there was a suit which looked fairly respectable. It fitted me pretty well, and in the natural order of things we began haggling again. Fifty *francs* changed hands.

Then I gave the Ghetto man another gold piece.

"Now hurry up and get me a hat somewhere, a pair of boots, a collar and a tie."

But here the fat old woman with her shrill voice began to make difficulties. I was bringing misfortune on them. It was after business hours anyway. I must not stay in the house any longer it was far too dangerous. "*Allez vous en—allez vous en!*"

The old lady began to get on my nerves, and I went willingly enough. At the corner I waited for the old Jew. In ten minutes he came back, and said that he could for twenty *francs* get me a really good outfit, boots, an extra collar, a good hat and a pair of gloves; for an extra twenty he could procure an excellent revolver. He got the money, and after a short time came back with two bundles.

At the end of the next street there was the high wall of the fortifications. From the inside I could climb over easily enough. The drop to the ground on the other side was a pretty big one, but I landed unhurt in the sand, in the middle of a palm grove. From the open windows of a villa close to the grove a flood of light streamed, and I could hear the merry sounds of a waltz. I could see the couples dancing. Many officers were amongst them. But there was no danger of being seen; it was pitch dark among the palms. In feverish haste I tore off my uniform and put on the civilian clothes. They fitted me well. It was quite a strange feeling fastening a collar and tie once more. . . .

And when I had changed I nailed uniform and overcoat, and boots and belt, and everything to a palm with the bayonet, wondering who would find them in the morning!

I drew on my gloves and my toilet was complete. In the villa the band (it was the Legion's band too) was playing a German waltz: "*Das ist das süsse Mädel. . . .*"

With a feeling very much akin to fright I walked to the nearest gate in the fortification walls. The soldiers on guard there, however, did not take the slightest notice of me. This gave me more confidence. Slowly and unostentatiously I crossed the promenade as though I were merely a respectable citizen out for a stroll. *Légionnaires* were promenading everywhere. More than once I had to turn and make a detour to avoid meeting non-commissioned officers of my own company. It was an exciting walk. At last I had passed through the main streets and came to a suburban road leading straight to the railway station. The little station was quite deserted. I looked carefully about me to see whether anybody was watching me, and then climbed down the steep embankment to the railroad tracks, leading straight to the north to Oran.

In the meantime it had become quite dark. From afar the lights of the station and of the switch-signals were shining; the lines themselves lay hidden in pitch-darkness. I began to run. At first I kept stumbling over the sharp stones between the rails and once I fell at full length. Soon, however, I got the hang of the thing, springing from sleeper to sleeper. I ran as hard as I could. A quarter of an hour, half an hour. Then I had to stop, coughing and out of breath. It was beginning to drizzle. The landscape was cloaked in inky darkness and there was only a faint gleam of light on the horizon far behind me to show where Sidi-bel-Abbès lay. . . . As far as I could tell I must have covered about five *kilometres*.

My feet were paining me. I drew off one of my boots and found that there were long rows of nails sticking up inside and that the soles were damp with blood. I tore up my handkerchief and made a pad from the rags to cover the nails. But the horrible little monsters bored through even this. Anyhow, it was far better than before. I examined the revolver in my pocket and it was a pleasant surprise to find that it was a capital weapon, a Browning pistol. The old Jew, who certainly knew nothing about weapons, had, with the revolver, atoned for his sins in the matter of boots!

Once more I started forward. My feet had to get accustomed to the nails whether they liked it or not. From now on I kept up an alternate double and walk, husbanding my strength as I had learnt to do in the Legion, running five minutes at the double and then walking five minutes, always following the railway's bee-line for the north. Once I heard the roar of a train behind me and lay down flat in the sand by the rails. Thus hour after hour went by. I had already passed three stations, which merely consisted of a few houses which lay there deserted in the darkness. As I passed a lonely signal-house a dog began to bark and I started off in deadly terror, running like a madman till I had left the beast tearing at his chain far behind me.

How thankful I was for the silence and darkness. . . . I breathed with difficulty, I had been running so hard. My clothes were soaked with sweat, and when I stopped for a moment to rest, an icy shiver passed over my whole body. But I pulled myself together, for I wanted to reach a medium- sized station, where it would not be so noticeable when I took a ticket for Oran.

The rain soon stopped again. And now the moon began to shine fitfully through the gaps in the clouds, even this faint light being much more than I cared about. A terrible fear of being seen by a police patrol came over me. All at once the country became hilly. On either side of the rails there lay mighty rocks, great jagged boulders of sandstone, and I rejoiced in the shelter they gave me. I had been running for some minutes between the rocks when I heard a strange noise. At first I thought it was another train. But as the sound grew nearer and grew clearer I knew what it was: galloping horses!

Through a gap in the rocks I could see the fine white line which marked the road. It was scarcely a hundred yards away from the railway. On this road a patrol was coming along at a gallop. . . .

Had the police already seen me? Just before, where the country was flat, my silhouette must have stood out sharply defined against the sky in the moonlight.

In a paroxysm of fear I crawled in between two rocks and held my breath to listen. The horses drew nearer and nearer, the beat of their hoofs on the roadway ringing out loud and clear. Peeping out of my hiding-place I could see the dark forms of horses and their riders. Now they were up with me. I heard a sharp exclamation in Arabic. The three men pulled up their horses and came to a halt.

I pulled out my pistol. The barrel shone in the moonlight. I hastily covered up the weapon with my coat, for fear it should betray my hiding-place. Then I carefully cocked the pistol and felt whether the cartridge-frame was in order. A feeling of icy calmness came upon me. I made up my mind not to stir from my hiding-place and not to fire until the *gendarmes* were quite close to me in their search. I considered the matter carefully. Two full cartridge-frames I took in my left hand, ready to refill the chamber. My idea was to empty the magazine in quick shooting in order to get in as many shots as possible before they recovered from their surprise.

Down below someone lit a match. It burned for a moment only. I heard one of the *gendarmes* laugh. Then the three men galloped forward again.

One of them must have asked his comrades for a match. . . .

The noise of the galloping horses was soon lost in the distance, but for a long time I sat trembling from head to foot between the two rocks. The tears of over-excitement were running down my face as I put up the pistol. I could have yelled for joy that this awful danger was over. When I stood up again, I fell back against the rocks. My trembling knees could not support my body. . . .

Les Imberts was the name of the station. It was forty-two *kilometres* distant from Sidi-bel-Abbès; in seven hours I had covered a distance of about thirty English miles. When at four o'clock in the morning I reached the station and deciphered its name and its distance from Sidi-bel-Abbès in the darkness, there was not a human being to be seen. The stillness of night still lay upon everything. A few hundred yards from the station a number of freight cars stood. I jumped into one of them and studied, lighting one match after another, the Algerian timetable which my careful mother had sent me. The first train to Oran went at a few minutes past five.

The first thing to be done was to care for my outer man a little. I climbed out of the car again and found, after a long search, a barrel half full of water standing under a shed. Day was just breaking. After a very hurried wash I hid again in one of the cars, brushing my clothes and cleaning my boots with my handkerchief. I was very glad of the extra collar which my friend of the Ghetto had purchased. Finally I had a look at myself in my tiny looking-glass. It would do! Indeed, the effect was not half bad. It would do very well; decently dressed people were scarce in Algeria. . . .

At five o'clock I started on a roundabout route for the station. A dozen people stood waiting on the platform, amongst them an Arab policeman leaning lazily against the wall. I went straight up to the ticket office.

"*Oran—premiere classe!*"

"*Sept-soixante,*" said the official. "Seven *francs* and sixty *centimes.*"

I jumped into the nearest first-class compartment, and found to my joy that it was empty. The train started off. During the two hours' journey from Les Imberts to Oran I brought my dress into decent order and smoked innumerable cigarettes to drive away my sleepiness. At the barrier in Oran a sergeant of *Zouaves* and a corporal of the Legion were watching for deserters, but they didn't take the slightest notice of me.

Until ten o'clock I wandered about the town. Then I went to the office of the French Mediterranean line and took a second-class ticket for Marseilles. The passenger boat *St. Augustine* was due to start at five in the afternoon.

All at once I became very sleepy. I could hardly keep my eyes open, but I had not the courage to go to an hotel and rest there for a few hours. So I went into a restaurant and enjoyed a long-drawn-out French dinner and a bottle of heavy Burgundy. Suddenly I remembered that it would look suspicious if I started on a sea voyage without any luggage. For a few *francs* I procured a big valise whose paste-board sides looked really "the same as leather," and bought newspapers at every corner to stuff my "luggage" with.

At a few minutes to five I went on board the steamer. With a cigarette between my lips and a bundle of newspapers under my arm I walked up and down the deck, read *Le Rire*, and did all I could to assume a careless mien. In reality I was in a very serious situation. The question was: Had a telegram from the regiment with my description reached Oran already or not?

The half-hour struck, but the *St. Augustine* was still in dock. Police came and went. All at once I felt myself go pale as death; a patrol of four *Zouave* sergeants was coming up the gangway. They went over the whole ship, looking carefully about them. Then they interchanged a few words with the captain and went on again. . . .

I was just beginning to breathe again, when a *gendarme* came up to me and asked, saluting courteously:

"*Monsieur is a Frenchman?*"

"*Non, monsieur*, an Englishman," I answered quietly, and smiled at the *gendarme* in spite of the icy fear gripping at my heart.

If he should chance on the idea of asking for my papers I was lost!

"Your name, please?"

"Eugene Sanders."

"Profession?"

"Engineer—from Tlemcen—on the way to Nice."

"Thank you."

...After a few minutes the ship's bell rang out, the gangways were pulled in, and the screw began to revolve. I went into my cabin and went to sleep. During the whole of the sea voyage I had not a single thought, not a single hope, not a single fear—I merely slept.

As the *St. Augustine* ran into harbour in Marseilles, a new difficulty presented itself. What would the custom-house say to my valise filled with paper? Luggage of this sort would have made anybody suspicious.

Chance came to my aid. A number of boats crowded around the ship, and several boatmen climbed on board to offer their services as porters, and so on. I went up to one of them and told him that I wanted to be put on shore as quickly as possible. Could he do it?

"For five *francs*," the fellow said.

"All right. Row me over."

My satchel I left on board to avoid the customs inspection.

A gangway had already been let down from the side of the steamer, and I stepped down into the boat with my boatman. Ten minutes later I stood on the *quai* in Marseilles. In another five minutes I had found a cab and was on my way to the station. Half an hour later I was seated in a compartment of an express train for the Riviera.

A Riviera journey in the darkness. . . . Toulon flew past—Cannes. In Nice I could hear even in the railway-train the noise of the carnival which was nearing its end—the platform was covered with confetti. We reached Monaco—Monte Carlo, with its brilliantly illuminated casino.

At last we reached Ventimiglia: the first Italian station!

It was one o'clock in the morning. I stormed into the telegraph-office and despatched two telegrams to my two dearest. . . .

Free—free again!

CHAPTER 15

J'accuse

Two years have passed.

They were years of fighting and years of toil. Years in which I burnt much midnight oil, and in which every tiny success meant worlds to me. My personal attitude towards the Foreign Legion was a rather peculiar one at first. For several months I forced myself never even to think of the time when I was in the Legion. Those times should merely be to me a dim shadow of the past.

I looked upon them as an ugly page that I should only too gladly have torn out of the book of my life: since, however, I could not rid myself of them in this way I avoided ever opening the book at this page. . . . But the past which we should like to forget has an unpleasant way of forcing itself upon us, unbidden and against our will.

Often as I lay back in my armchair in an idle quarter of an hour, scenes from my life in the Legion mingled dimly with the blue smoke of my cigarette. An endless procession of *légionnaires* would pass before me, a procession of men loaded like beasts of burden, their backs bent almost double, panting and gasping as they struggled forward in the sand: I could see their staring eyes, their rounded backs. I felt the tortures they were undergoing, how they struggled forward till their last ounce of strength was spent: even their groans were audible to me.

Every one of these men seemed to look at me with hatred. You sit there in your armhair? In an atmosphere of culture? Amongst beautiful things of art? You belong to us! Off to your place, *légionnaire*, on the wing of the first row of fours in the eleventh company. Quick march, *légionnaire*, or die! When I spent a golden coin on some amusement I seemed to see the hands of the *légionnaires*, trembling claw-like hands, grasping for my money and trying to rend it from me. Gold! Wealth unheard of after the miserable coppers of the Legion! Give it to us, said those fingers, give it to us! Have you forgotten our five *centimes*, *légionnaire*?

My imagination worried me.

I gave a part of the story of my life price, and after much hesitation wrote this book. I have only described the ordinary routine of life in the regiment of foreigners as I myself experienced it. It is merely a tiny part of what every *légionnaire* undergoes.

I wanted to show the *légionnaire*—how he lives, and how he must work. I did not dream of being able to warn foolish young fellows about the Legion. It is impossible to warn a fool. But I thought, and think still, that a true and exact description of the French Foreign Legion would perhaps help to put an end to an institution which is a disgrace to civilised humanity, and which should be to the civilised nations of to-day as unintelligible as the slave trade. . . . And above all I wanted to get rid of those visions which troubled me.

In considering the Foreign Legion one must above all be careful not to go to work with common-places, nor to start from general axioms. The idea is so prevalent that the soldiers of the Foreign Legion are lost and ruined men, even criminals morally and practically useless at best. A good-for-nothing lot of fellows who are no loss to anybody.

One is apt to dispose of the *légionnaire* in a few trite remarks. Men of learning write from their armchairs to the papers about "the hirelings who have sold themselves into slavery, thus helping to revive the feudal system of the Middle Ages." If, however, the question were more closely inquired into, I am sure that it would be found that these rogues and vagabonds are not, in reality, quite so bad. True, I can bring forward no positive proof of this. There are no statistics about the Foreign Legion, and I am in no better position than any other human being to bring forward authentic material. There are not even official figures about the strength of the two regiments.

I admit, willingly enough, that a large percentage of the men in the Foreign Legion really deserve the callous summing up that one is wont to apply to the whole regiment. All that I have seen and heard in Africa, however, has convinced me that the other and greater part of the men in the Foreign Legion are anything but the lost souls one imagines them to be. They come into the Legion as poor workmen. Their story is the sad one of the vagabond workman who had to starve on the French high road, because he could not speak the language. It is these men who have always formed the heart of the

Foreign Legion. It is the pangs of hunger that drives men into the Foreign Legion—French and English, Germans and Italians, Spaniards and Austrians, men of all countries, men of all races. Yes, hunger is a most efficient recruiting sergeant for the Foreign Legion.

The hungry man who seeks a refuge in the Foreign Legion gets, it is true, his daily bread; he is, all the same, disgracefully swindled. It cannot be repeated often enough how hard the *légionnaire* has to work, how miserable his existence is, how he gives his whole strength for a wage that is not worth mentioning. We are so practical in our modern ideas of life; every workman knows well enough the exact value of his work in the current coin of the realm, and takes advantage of every opportunity of getting a higher wage. And, in an age which is ever improving the standard of living, and which has so absolutely changed the ideas of the poorer classes, how is it possible that a business concern like the Foreign Legion—it is really nothing but a business concern, a commercial undertaking—can always get hundreds and thousands of labourer-soldiers, for a wage compared with which the wages of the tiniest village are riches?

The results are startling when one compares the Foreign Legion with the world's two other mercenary armies, those of America and England, both of which countries, by-the-by, take great care to keep up a certain moral standard among their soldiers. These two armies, in sharp contrast to the Foreign Legion, pay their soldiers exceptionally well. The least that an American regular receives is thirteen dollars a month; the English Tommy gets a shilling a day. And these are soldiers and not workmen. They are mercenaries, like the *légionnaire*, but at any rate they are well-paid mercenaries.

The miserable wages, together with the existing conditions of life in the Legion, are enough to convince even a Frenchman that the existence of the Foreign Legion is a sin against the very first principles of humanity—and has been for eighty years. In the sand of Algeria, in the swamps of Madagascar, in the fever-pested plains of Tonquin, in the valleys of Mexico, there lie these men of every nation, these men who have died in the Foreign Legion, who have sold their lives for their rations and five *centimes* a day.

If one leaves the dead in peace and only considers the living, one reaches the same conclusion: robbery, and robbery of the destitute at that! A sin against every principle of humanity! Oh, thrice accursed Legion: forcing inexperienced young fellows into its ranks, who would never join did they know what lies before them; absolutely callous as to the value of human life, forcing its soldiers to conditions of life which must ruin their health forever!

It is not for this alone that the Legion is answerable. It is also answerable for the vices of the Legion, for it is the life in the Legion that has brought the tiny seeds of these vices to full bloom.

About the political aspect of the Foreign Legion there can be no two opinions.

The Foreign Legion is an antiquated, ridiculously out-of-date survival of the feudal system of the Middle Ages, with all the disadvantages of the mercenary system, but without the romantic halo which in days gone by hung around the soldiers of fortune.

According to modern ideas, it is absolutely monstrous that one of the most cultured nations of the world should have in its pay a corps composed of men of all nationalities, and who are, as is generally acknowledged, very often foreign deserters, who enlist to save themselves from starvation. Their colours bear the unsatisfying motto, "*Valeur et Discipline*." The inscription on the national flag, "*Honneur et Patrie*"—"For Honour and our Country"—could hardly be given to these "mixed pickles." But these two words, "*Valeur*" and "Discipline," are pregnant with meaning. Comparisons with the English and American armies are not only of interest as far as the pay is concerned; there is in all respects a vast difference between these two armies and the Foreign Legion.

Only men of British birth can join the British army. The American army takes foreigners into its ranks, but only those who possess the so-called first papers, *i.e.*, have sworn before a magistrate that they intend to become American citizens after the prescribed five years. The American mercenary is looked upon as an American citizen and has to take the oath of allegiance. The Foreign Legion, on the other hand, knows no oath at all. The printed bit of paper that the recruit for the Foreign Legion signs is merely a contract, a statement of the conditions of service. This contract is the only chain which fetters the *légionnaire* to the Legion—a contract which, according to every one of our modern ideas of international law, is null and void.

Today, (as at first publication), in international law, contracts opposed to public morality are much talked about, and what could be more immoral in every sense of the word than this contract that the French Republic makes with its recruits, this contract in which what is got out of a man and what he is paid stand in such an unsatisfying relation to each other.

As I have said before, there can be no two opinions about the Foreign Legion. Every one with sound ideas of political economy must agree that it is an unheard-of condition of affairs when a nation is allowed to receive the deserters and criminals—I speak now of that other half of the Foreign Legion of the States surrounding it, indeed from all the States in the world, with open arms, and to make use of them on principle for a special military organisation. One cannot speak too strongly about this transaction, which is a piece of military blackguardism with something more than despicable about it.

And not only the feudalism of the Middle Ages survives in the Foreign Legion but also the morals of those times, when a poor devil enlisted because he did not know of anything better to do with his life: of those times when a deserter was valued because he made a pair of arms and legs the less in the opposing force. In the Foreign Legion's enlistment *bureaux* a recruit gets a special welcome when he announces that he is a deserter, and is then looked upon as a really valuable addition to the corps.

It is also a fact that France offers sanctuary to all criminals who fly from justice. The Foreign Legion will only give up murderers—every other kind of criminal is safe there. And France's selfish reason for this is that she can thereby fill the ranks of a regiment that is always fighting for France and which is always ready to do the hardest work for her in the most unhealthy climates. The average Frenchman has, during the Legion's eighty years of existence, contented himself with attributing the successes of the Foreign Legion to the French flag, and has always looked upon the Foreign Legion as a profitable and patriotic institution. It is only quite of late that the Foreign Legion has come to be looked upon in France as a problem.

Today, (at time of first publication), the Foreign Legion is not an institution that every Frenchman considers quite in the natural order of things. Even the French Ministry of War has busied itself with the "Legion problem." It could not, however, quite make up its mind to give up the Legion. The possibility of employing a soldier who receives five *centimes* a day, and who can be made use of for all sorts of dangerous undertakings in the worst of climates, is too great a temptation.

Perhaps the real reason for this tenacity is that France, who is so proud of her military traditions, finds, it hard to bring herself to dissolve a corps which has been in existence for more than eighty years and which has been led by many a famous general and marshal of

France.

It has been suggested that it would be a good idea to change the method of recruiting. Passports should be demanded to make sure that the recruit had not got into trouble with the authorities of his own country. Deserters from the armies of other countries should on no condition be accepted.

There is a diversity of opinion about these suggestions in French military circles. One party asserts that with the deserters the Foreign Legion would lose the flower of its strength, the soldiers who have been trained in other armies. The other side urges that if the pay were raised and the time the men must serve in order to qualify for a pension shortened, the adventurous life in the Foreign Legion and the hope of promotion would always bring more than enough good stuff from all nations for service under the Legion's flag. In these debates the military point of view is the only one of importance and since, considered from this point of view, the Legion has always borne itself splendidly, things have been left as they were. All suggestions for a change in the organisation of the Legion have naturally been made very quietly. All the same the Legion has, of late, (at time of first publication), come very much before the public in France.

There is no doubt that they are beginning to look at the Foreign Legion a little critically in France. The number of those who doubt that the country is right in keeping up this barbarous institution is growing daily. Referring to the great mutiny of the soldiers of the Legion at Saida, Jaurès wrote in the *Humanité*:

> The Foreign Legion will doubtless be a source of everlasting difficulty to us; the idea of forming a body of troops for the French army from foreign deserters is at any rate an unusual one.

This is a step in the right direction. They are beginning to talk about the problem of the Foreign Legion. Its existence is no longer considered absolutely natural. The question has been raised. If the Foreign Legion did not exist, and some member of the French parliament were to suggest the formation of a corps of foreign mercenaries, preferably foreign deserters, the suggestion would doubtless be received with indignation. The tactless politician would be sure to be confronted with the somewhat obvious remark that it would be unworthy of the dignity of France to gather a band of foreigners under the tricolour to defend French soil.

One would hear some very pretty speeches on the subject. That sort of thing can be tolerated in the Balkan States or in Venezuela or Honduras, but not in our proud France. Some deputy or other would be certain to warn the nation the warning is a very obvious one— that other States could institute Foreign Legions, filling their ranks with French deserters. Think of the shudder that would pass through the land at the idea of English ships manned by, or German colonies conquered by, French deserters.

The Foreign Legion lives upon its past. The Frenchman is accustomed to it and hardly notices what an anachronism it is.

The problem of the Legion is so easy. It can be divided into two questions:

Is it fair to pay a man who works really hard a daily wage of five *centimes*?

Is it fair to make use of a poor devil's misfortunes, or the fact that he has got into trouble with the authorities of his native land, in this way for national purposes?

The answer to these questions is not difficult.

In later years especially, the French Government has made a clean sweep of many French institutions that seemed to be incompatible with the fair fame of France. One can be quite sure that it will in course of time be recognised that the Foreign Legion must be done away with.

One is only tempted to ask: How long will it last?

Quousque tandem . . .?

LEONAUR

ALSO FROM LEONAUR

AVAILABLE IN SOFTCOVER OR HARDCOVER WITH DUST JACKET

THE 9TH—THE KING'S (LIVERPOOL REGIMENT) IN THE GREAT WAR 1914 - 1918 *by Enos H. G. Roberts*—Mersey to mud—war and Liverpool men.

THE GAMBARDIER *by Mark Severn*—The experiences of a battery of Heavy artillery on the Western Front during the First World War.

FROM MESSINES TO THIRD YPRES *by Thomas Floyd*—A personal account of the First World War on the Western front by a 2/5th Lancashire Fusilier.

THE IRISH GUARDS IN THE GREAT WAR - VOLUME 1 *by Rudyard Kipling*—Edited and Compiled from Their Diaries and Papers—The First Battalion.

THE IRISH GUARDS IN THE GREAT WAR - VOLUME 1 *by Rudyard Kipling*—Edited and Compiled from Their Diaries and Papers—The Second Battalion.

ARMOURED CARS IN EDEN *by K. Roosevelt*—An American President's son serving in Rolls Royce armoured cars with the British in Mesopatamia & with the American Artillery in France during the First World War.

CHASSEUR OF 1914 *by Marcel Dupont*—Experiences of the twilight of the French Light Cavalry by a young officer during the early battles of the great war in Europe.

TROOP HORSE & TRENCH *by R.A. Lloyd*—The experiences of a British Lifeguardsman of the household cavalry fighting on the western front during the First World War 1914-18.

THE EAST AFRICAN MOUNTED RIFLES *by C.J. Wilson*—Experiences of the campaign in the East African bush during the First World War.

THE LONG PATROL *by George Berrie*—A Novel of Light Horsemen from Gallipoli to the Palestine campaign of the First World War.

THE FIGHTING CAMELIERS *by Frank Reid*—The exploits of the Imperial Camel Corps in the desert and Palestine campaigns of the First World War.

STEEL CHARIOTS IN THE DESERT *by S. C. Rolls*—The first world war experiences of a Rolls Royce armoured car driver with the Duke of Westminster in Libya and in Arabia with T.E. Lawrence.

WITH THE IMPERIAL CAMEL CORPS IN THE GREAT WAR *by Geoffrey Inchbald*—The story of a serving officer with the British 2nd battalion against the Senussi and during the Palestine campaign.

Lightning Source UK Ltd.
Milton Keynes UK
172954UK00001B/236/P